DISCARD

What Others Are Saying about Roxane Battle and *Pockets of Joy*

"Transforming pain into power is possible. In *Pockets of Joy*, Roxane shows us how to tap into our unlimited potential and keep our spirits rising."

—*Tavis Smiley*
National talk show host
New York Times best-selling author
Time magazine's "The World's 100 Most Influential People"

"What a joy to read! Roxane's charisma shines through every page. *Pockets of Joy* is a precious gift that has the power to inspire, nourish, and bless each reader. Read this book and be transformed!"

—*Gregory A. Plotnikoff, MD, MTS, FACP*
Co-author, *Trust Your Gut*

"It takes people years to understand and find their passion. Many never find their own *Pockets of Joy*. Roxane Battle shares her journey and the path she chose to take as a single mother pursuing a successful career. *Pockets of Joy* will inspire and motivate you in making decisions to be happy and free. Her story is a remarkable one...it will not only enrich you, it will inspire you."

—*Pam Borton*
President & CEO, Borton Partners
Speaker, author of *On Point*
Winningest coach in University of Minnesota women's basketball history

"*Pockets of Joy* will remind you that you were born to be joy-full. Your joy-tank came full. Life has a way of burning the joy-fuel but it also provides opportunities to fill the joy-tank and keep it full. May you have many pockets and may they all be bulging with joy."

—*Sam Chand*
Leadership Consultant
Author, *Leadership Pain*
www.SamChand.com

"In this delightfully honest book, we cheer for Roxane as she makes difficult and wise choices in an effort to forge work-life balance. Her refreshing example in our success-crazed culture is an inspiration to women and men everywhere!"

—*Deborah Smith Pegues*
International speaker
Best-selling author, *30 Days to Taming Your Tongue*

"Pockets of Joy briefly recounts Roxane's divorce and her departure from television news, focusing largely on the next chapter of her life as a single mom. A deeply spiritual person, Battle counts her belief that things would and could get better among the reasons she was able to move on."

—*Caryn Sullivan*
Award-winning columnist
Author, *Bitter or Better*

"*Pockets of Joy* is for anyone who has experienced that deep realization that life hasn't gone the way they planned. It's for anyone who never expected to end up where they are. It's for anyone who's thinking about giving up. If that's you, then this is the book you need right now."

—*Kathleen Cooke*
Cofounder, Cooke Pictures and Influence Lab

"*Pockets of Joy* is candidly, beautifully written, and easy to read. It is Roxane's story of finding those 'pockets of joy' during an extremely difficult season in her life. Whether you're a single mom or not, you will find yourself quickly drawn into it, and learning invaluable life lessons along the way."

—*Janet Conley*
Pastor, Cottonwood Church
Los Alamitos, California

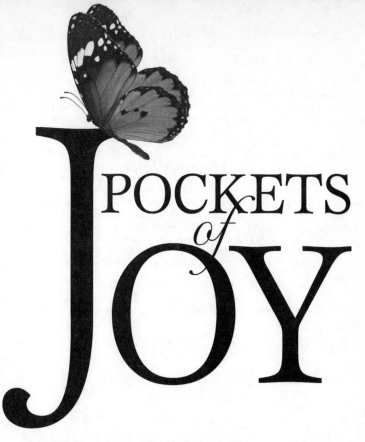

POCKETS *of* JOY

Deciding to Be Happy, Choosing to Be Free

ROXANE BATTLE

WHITAKER
HOUSE

Publisher's Note:
Some names have been changed to protect the privacy of the individuals.

Unless otherwise marked, all Scripture quotations marked (NKJV) are taken from the *New King James Version*, © 1979, 1980, 1982 by Thomas Nelson, Inc. Used by permission. All rights reserved. Scripture quotations marked (NLT) are taken from the *Holy Bible, New Living Translation*, © 1996. Used by permission of Tyndale House Publishers, Inc., Carol Stream, Illinois 60188. All rights reserved. Scripture quotations marked (MSG) are taken from *The Message: The Bible in Contemporary Language* by Eugene H. Peterson, © 1993, 1994, 1995, 1996, 2000, 2001, 2002. Used by permission of NavPress Publishing Group. All rights reserved. Represented by Tyndale House Publishers, Inc. Scripture quotations marked (NIV) are taken from the *Holy Bible, New International Version*®, NIV®, © 1973, 1978, 1984, 2011 by Biblica, Inc.® Used by permission of Zondervan. All rights reserved worldwide. www.zondervan.com. The "NIV" and "New International Version" are trademarks registered in the United States Patent and Trademark Office by Biblica, Inc. Scripture quotation noted (CEB) is taken from the Common English Bible, copyright 2011. Used by permission. All rights reserved. Scripture quotations marked (GW) are taken from *God's Word*®, © 1995 by God's Word to the Nations. Used by permission of Baker Publishing Group. Boldface type in the Scripture quotations indicates the author's emphasis.

POCKETS OF JOY:
Deciding to Be Happy, Choosing to Be Free

roxane@roxanebattle.com

ISBN: 978-1-62911-910-6
eBook ISBN: 978-1-62911-911-3
Printed in the United States of America
© 2017 by Roxane Battle

Whitaker House
1030 Hunt Valley Circle
New Kensington, PA 15068
www.whitakerhouse.com

Library of Congress record available at https://lccn.loc.gov/2017027934

1 2 3 4 5 6 7 8 9 10 11 ⨀ 24 23 22 21 20 19 18 17

CONTENTS

To my parents,
Burnie and Bessie,
and everyone who has ever
encouraged me to dream big.

PART I:
THE POCKETS

Introduction

METAMORPHOSIS

When your faith is tested, your endurance has a chance to grow.
So let it grow, for when your endurance is fully developed, you will
be perfect and complete, needing nothing.
—James 1:3–4 NLT

Some years ago, while working as a news reporter for a television station in Minneapolis, I got the assignment of a lifetime: follow the trek of the migrating monarch butterfly to Mexico.

Each year the monarch travels two thousand miles from Minnesota to overwinter high up in the cool mountains of central Mexico. The butterflies gather there and hibernate, hanging like enormous clusters of fruit from the boughs of fir trees, and if you listen closely you will hear the flapping of a million pairs of wings as they set flight, momentarily darkening the sky with their collective mass.

I and a talented photojournalist named Greg flew to Mexico, along with a seventh grade science class from suburban Minneapolis, and I got to witness all of this with my own eyes. Our destination was a little-known butterfly sanctuary positioned high up in the mountains surrounding the town of Angangueo, a tiny village nestled in the slopes of volcanic highlands, some 280 kilometers northwest of Mexico City and deep in the heart of Mexico.

We climbed up the mountain, first on foot, then by horseback, as a constant trickle of monarchs fluttered about us much like a light shower of fluffy snowflakes, occasionally lighting on our shoulders and hair. The butterflies increased in number the closer we got to the top of the mountain until we reached a clearing in a forest of oyamel trees. There, monarch butterflies hung from branches like leaves by the thousands as far as the eye could see.

How is it that they prevail across trade winds, finding their way across continents and returning to the exact same spot each year, generation after generation? How could so much internal guidance be packed into such a tiny creature?

I interviewed our tour guide who told me that she, along with others in the Mexican culture, believe monarchs are the messengers of God. They are most certainly His creation, perhaps created to remind us of this one thing: perseverance. For without perseverance, the monarch butterfly would cease to be. From its beginning stage as a lowly larva inching along the ground, to a chrysalis-covered pupa, it transforms its entire being through patience and time, finally emerging to dry its amber-hued wings in the warm sunlight and soar freely above the earth as an adult butterfly.

Just the sight of a monarch reminds me of possibilities in the face of what might not otherwise be. Looking back over my life, it would be easy to simply state that my faith is what has sustained me through difficult times. And yes, much like the monarch, a force greater than myself sustains my life. Yet unlike the monarch, whose metamorphosis is purely instinctive, without variance or choice, I have a choice and so do you. We have a choice to keep going or give up. To acknowledge the possibilities, to adapt to inevitable change, or to dig our heels in and refuse to grow. To let current situations determine future outcomes or to persevere toward what we want, toward what will bring us joy.

In the end we have our faith. And we also have a choice.

Imagine soaring freely like a monarch high above the earth, fluttering over majestic vistas, oceans, and plains. A sight it never would have seen had the monarch remained in its initial state.

As human beings we instinctively resist change. It brings uncertainty and, often, sorrow. It is more comforting to remain as we are than to seek or embrace the unknown. But I have found that if we are ever to find joy in life, we must be willing to face the changing circumstances of life with courage and a belief that, though difficult, it all works out in the end. That's the reason why butterflies are so very special to me. I have images of them on my stationery, teacups, plates, and pajamas, and you will find them floating through the pages of this book as a reminder to persevere, to press on toward that which you are destined to do despite headwinds and the uncertainty of the lengthy journey ahead.

Perseverance is an outward expression of possibility. Throughout my life, even from a very young age, I have always persevered in finding the glass to be half-full, not half-empty. For others in my life, maybe not so much. I just could never figure out why my happiness apparently left some folks in my life annoyed. I remember singing in the church choir when I was around eleven or twelve. I had already discovered a love for writing and knew, after seeing Barbara Walters on one of her television specials interviewing some young starlet poolside, that I wanted to be a journalist on television. And so I was thrilled when our church choir was asked to be a part of my uncle's television show. One weeknight each month, a few select choir members including me and my four brothers would go down to the local ABC affiliate and tape four half-hour episodes of a religious television program. We'd sing a song at the beginning, my uncle the pastor would deliver a fifteen-minute sermonette, and we'd sing another song at the end. That was it.

14

The program aired on Sunday mornings at 5:00 a.m. My mom, dad, and brothers would still be fast asleep, but I'd creep downstairs to the living room in my jammies wrapped in a blanket, and park on the floor in front of the television set with the volume turned down low, hoping to hear and see myself on TV. And wouldn't you know it, every now and then, between a "hallelujah" or "thank you Jesus," there I was on a tight shot, in a lime green polyester choir robe with billowing sleeves, just smiling and singing away, looking right into the camera. So much so, the choir director eventually moved me to the back row.

A few years later, while pursuing a degree in broadcast journalism, I found myself in front of another lens and painfully aware of how overt optimism can at times be misplaced. I was a freshman at the University of Minnesota–Twin Cities, taking an intro to broadcast journalism class. My assignment was to prepare and deliver a mock weather forecast. The whole set-up was primitive to say the least: an outline of the United States drawn in chalk on a blackboard. Little light blue raindrops symbolized rain on the Eastern seaboard, and a yellow sun indicated a warming trend to the south. I wore a dark blue suit and a big smile, looked right into the camera, pointed to the map, and had fun pretending to be the weather girl. On the day of my critique, my classmates' consensus was that I appeared to be a bit "too happy" about the weather!

Years later during the early years of my television career, my bosses had varying opinions on my hair styles or clothes but all agreed on one thing. Again. Despite the fact that I could write well, had learned to read a teleprompter, and perfected the art of ad-libbing while live on location from a breaking news story, several news managers at the various TV stations actually told me that—get this—I *smiled too much*. I wasn't serious enough. Being too happy on the news was a problem, they said. I needed to be more serious. Or somber. Which was it? I guess having spent more than two decades on local television is testament to the fact that I eventually figured it out.

Yet to this day, for me, happiness is innate. An eternal optimist? Hopeless romantic? Pollyanna? Maybe all of those labels apply. To this day, I still believe that even in the midst of the muck and miry mess we call life, joy can be found.

Joy's precepts are perseverance, gratitude, and intentionality; practices that sustained me during a really crummy time in

15

my life. Yet, you won't hear me grousing. Instead, I've chosen to write about the sustaining power of this simple concept called joy. Imagine that—someone who has spent a lifetime annoying people with her optimism would go on to write a book about joy. That is exactly what I've done.

Like you, I'm on a journey, and this is my story—one I've never really shared publicly until now. Just like many of you, my life has been filled with both joy and heartache. I have done a lot and seen a lot and to be honest, I know I've been blessed—to live in the United States, to have gotten an education, to have succeeded at a profession, to have gotten married and given birth. Becoming a mother was the single most transformative event of my life. And within months of giving birth to our son, my husband and I divorced. The reasons are deeply personal and private. I want to be very clear from the very beginning that even though we divorced, my ex-husband was and continues to be an exemplary father to our son. This book isn't about our irreconcilable differences. Those are between us and, as such, will remain private.

What this book *is* about is the season in my life when I was on my own and overwhelmed with trying to put my life back together while I learned how to raise a child and navigate a demanding television career. A working, divorced single mom. That was me. For years. There were many days when I smiled in front of the camera and cried alone at night.

During those years, which I sometimes call my "time in the wilderness," I learned a lot about myself, and I am now at a point in my life when I can share the very personal and intimate stories of how I found peace in the midst of my struggles. What I call pockets. Pockets of joy.

The kind of joy that causes your eyes to mist and wash over the hurt. The kind of joy that catches you by surprise and for a moment makes you forget, if ever so briefly, that you ever felt pain. The kind of joy that, in some ways, can't even be described.

Yet in the pages that follow, I'm going to try.

1

P-A-I-N

*Whatever things are true, whatever things are noble, whatever things are just, **whatever things are pure**, whatever things are lovely, whatever things are of good report, if there is any virtue and if there is anything praiseworthy—meditate on these things.*
—Philippians 4:8

She stood in front of the room with a piece of chalk between her right thumb and index finger. It was an August evening, around 8:00 p.m. Flecks of dust danced in the light as the evening sun filtered through the miniblinds of a first-floor hospital conference room filled with gray folding chairs. On them were seated a dozen or more couples, each woman six to seven months pregnant.

"So," said the instructor, "when you think about childbirth, what's the first word that comes to your mind?"

It took but a second, and the answer came almost in unison.

"Pain!"

"Pain," she repeated in a stubborn Texas drawl that had resisted a decade or more of living in the Midwest.

"P-A-I-N." She wrote the letters on the green chalkboard. Underline.

Just as expected, *the instructor thought.* She'd taught these Lamaze classes for years, and each time she asked first-time parents that question, without fail, "pain" was the immediate answer. She turned and faced them again. Scanning the class with a chalky index finger, she asked, "What else?"

"Sleep deprivation."

"Yeah, no sleep," someone agreed.

Lack of sleep. Period. was now written on the board, underneath PAIN.

"Anything else?" she asked.

"How about stress?" someone ventured.

"Stress, you think of stress?"

"Yeah, stress is a good one," said a young, soon-to-be dad wearing a red silk tie loosened at the neck of a starched white cotton shirt that had looked a lot better a few hours ago.

"Okay," she said, "stress." *Stress* was now up on the chalkboard.

"What else?"

The men looked at the women; the women looked at the men; then, between them, a murmur of consideration.

"How about medications?"

"Meds are for the pain, and we already said that."

"Yeah, you're right."

"Well, gee, labor is part of childbirth."

"Labor is painful."

"And pain is already on the list, guys."

"Oh yeah, right. Sorry."

The instructor tucked her bottom lip under her upper front teeth. What she really wanted to do was bite her tongue. It's amazing, she thought, how a roomful of total strangers can think so much alike. Then, trying to keep a straight face, and in a tone that was unnaturally high, even for her, she asked, "Anything else?"

One pregnant woman in the front row shrugged. Her husband leaned forward with his elbows resting on his knees and his chin resting in his hands. He studied the list on the board one more time as if he were a contestant on a quiz show anticipating someone to declare, "Final answer!" Satisfied, he leaned back and rested his hands in his lap.

21

"That about covers it," he said.

"OK." It never fails, she thought.

"Look at this list. Pain. Lack of sleep and stress." She made a chalky check mark beside each item on the list and then prodded one more time.

"Is anything missing?"

Silence.

"Think!" she said.

Silence.

OK, *she thought,* just tell them.

"What about the end result? What do you get for all the pain, sleep deprivation, and stress? What about that beautiful little bay-be?!"

B-A-B-Y. Exclamation point. Underline. Underline. Happy face.

I was one of those first-time, expectant parents. Seven months and 160 pounds. I would gain five more pounds for a total of thirty-five before it was all said and done. My feet had swollen so much that the only shoes that fit were white Keds sneakers with the laces undone. I walked with a wobble, slept on my side, couldn't see my toes, and had lost all recollection of what it was like to bend over. All I wanted, all the time, were Burger King Whoppers with extra mustard.

My white rayon maternity top was starting to itch, and the belly panel on my black stretch pants refused to stretch anymore. My legs were twice their normal size. I didn't know it at the time but would soon learn that I had developed preeclampsia, a form of high blood pressure during pregnancy, which caused protein to spill into my urine. In other words, my body was poisoning itself. There would be a scramble at the end to save me and my baby. I would go on maternity leave with bed-rest a month before my due date. Concerned for my health, my doctor decided I needed to deliver early, eleven days early.

I was just grateful the swelling hadn't affected my face. Most of the television station's viewers didn't even know that I was

22

pregnant, except when the cameras caught me on a wide shot when I was out in the field reporting. The switchboard at the TV station got calls from viewers trying to confirm the obvious. But, thankfully, I spent the last few months of my pregnancy in the studio, where the cameras went in tight and shot me from the shoulders up. Reading the news was an easy job for a pregnant lady, except when I had to get up at 3:00 a.m. to fill in on the 6:00 a.m. news.

I had endured months of morning sickness—scratch that—evening sickness. I loved food, especially dinner: sweet-and-sour chicken, vegetable stir-fry, moo goo gai pan, and yeah, a Whopper or two. Dinners started out with an almost crazed expectation of satiating my hunger but ended with a frantic dash to the bathroom and tears. I was so hungry all the time, but in those first few months, I couldn't keep anything down. We had long since abandoned eating out. Heartburn, weight gain, and fatigue had all visited me those last seven months and I was ready for it to be over. I had cried and complained, until that night at Lamaze class.

Several people in the class were still holding on to white Styrofoam cups filled with melting ice cubes and watery red punch left over from the class break. The brownies and chocolate-chip cookies had quickly disappeared. The relish tray sat, picked over. A few of the moms-to-be, including myself, had taken an obligatory carrot stick or broccoli spear because, after all, we were supposed to be eating healthy. But what we really wanted was chocolate in any form. I took a sip of my punch and looked at the board, then looked around the room. It was something to see a roomful of adults staring at the chalkboard, looking guilty.

23

B-A-B-Y. Exclamation point. Underline. Underline. Happy face.

Of course, the baby, that wonderful bundle of joy. I was about to behold a miracle. Yet my husband and I, like the rest of the couples in the room, were filled with fear.

Fear of what was to come.

Fear of what we didn't know.

Fear of the uncertainty ahead.

Fear that led us down a path of negativity.

It's going to hurt. We'll never sleep. How will we adjust?

"What about the bay-be?!"

24

Yes, what about the baby? What about the joy? That night in the Lamaze class I learned to start looking for the joy. Yes, there may be stress and pain, but oh, what joy.

The first time I'd hear him cry, or see him smile.

Hold him in my arms. Oh, what unspeakable joy. Hope-filled expectation wrapped in a blanket and smelling like Johnson & Johnson.

There in the midst of so many negative emotions were pockets of joy. All I had to do was look for them, find them and gravitate toward them, embrace them, celebrate them, and lock them in my mind to remember during the times when the joy would be so hard to find.

I checked in to the hospital and was induced at 9:30 on a Thursday morning. My son was born the next day at 11:30 a.m. That's right; twenty-six hours of labor. I was basically awake the whole time. At first all I felt were sporadic, tiny little pulses and I would try to catch a quick nap in between. But with each passing hour the pulses and the pain in my abdomen deepened. I couldn't eat anything except Popsicles. My husband, sitting next to my hospital bed, would unwrap a Popsicle, break it in half, hand me one half, then sit silently at the edge of the bed sucking on the other.

While some women have an easy time getting pregnant and having children, I did not. I wanted a child very much, but I would discover that I had inherited my mother's genes that presented reproductive challenges for us both.

I was born one month premature, in the middle of a beautiful spring day in May. My mother was admiring an upstairs bedroom that had just been repainted robin's egg blue. The shade seemed appropriate at the time. After three boys, my mother and father just assumed the fourth would also be a boy. And so here she was, all of twenty-four years old, doing what most pregnant women do a month before delivery: nesting. Preparing a nursery that had already greeted three baby boys. It had all become routine. Without a thought she reached inside a closet to rearrange what was there, and that's when it hit: a pain so excruciating it brought her to the closet floor on her knees. It was all she could do to make it to the window and summon her five-year-old preschooler, my oldest brother BJ, who was playing in the yard below.

"Mommy is so sick, go tell Mrs. Walker to come here right quick," she instructed him. BJ made a mad dash to the neighbor's house, and within minutes Mrs. Walker had my mother into the back seat of her 1958 Buick. The five-minute drive to Charles T. Miller Hospital seemed like an eternity, the pain growing worse with each passing mile.

My mother was rushed through the front door, into emergency, and delivery. A scant six minutes later, I was born.

Four pounds and nine ounces.

Mrs. Walker had called my dad at work to tell him a baby was on the way.

"It can't be!" he had exclaimed over the phone. "The baby's not due for another month!"

"I'm tellin' you Burnie, the baby's coming and coming now!" Mrs. Walker had replied.

My father left work, went home, showered, changed out of his work clothes into a suit and tie, and headed for the hospital. He missed the delivery, but was thrilled with the news that greeted him when he got there.

"Oh my," said Dr. Hodgson, "we've got a girl this time!" Dr. Jane Hodgson had been there for the previous three births, as had the nurses. Three births, three boys.

Years later as my mother recounted the story of my birth, she told me how the nurse had laid me across her stomach and tagged my feet with a plastic band matching the one my mother already wore on her wrist.

"A girl?" my mother asked in disbelief. "Let me see."

The nurse held me up so that my mother could see the proof, and then they took me away. I was blue and had yet to make a sound. Instead of my mother's arms, or a bassinette in the hospital nursery, an isolette, back then called incubators, was where I spent my first four days on earth.

One month premature and underweight.

My parents hadn't seen me except for those few brief moments right after I was born, and they thought I was dead. My mother assumed the doctors and nurses were just sparing her the heartbreaking news.

"When can I see her?" she would ask.

"Oh, she's fine," they would reassure her. "You'll get to see her soon."

"Is she all right?"

"She's fine, just fine."

The truth was that my mother may have been closer to death than I was. She lost massive amounts of blood in the trauma surrounding my birth. The doctors advised my mother that it would be dangerous for her to have any more children—but she did. My parents had another boy, my baby brother Nate. Four boys: BJ, short for Burnie Jr., after my dad; Walter, Robert, and Nathanial,

27

all named after my uncles; and me, named after a model my mother had seen on TV.

I would grow up to look just like my father: fair-skinned, brown oval-shaped eyes, a square jaw line, and wide forehead with premature worry lines. My dad, a very tall man with large hands, was the first African-American with a master's electrician license in the state of Minnesota. While working as a department store janitor and at a meat packing house during the day, he went to night school for six years studying for his license exam. He got a near-perfect score and opened Battle Electric, a small storefront electrical contracting business located in the heart of the St. Paul's black community on the corner of University and Dale Avenue. Dad's contracting business is what put oatmeal and meatloaf on our table. I remember as a kid, my mom would take us by Dad's shop sometimes and we would look for the white bakery bag that sat on the counter in the reception area next to an hours-old pot of black coffee. My brothers and I would fight over what was left in the bag—a stale cake or jelly donut or leftover Danish.

Over time, as Dad's business grew, he'd add one or two more utility vans to a small fleet of white trucks with black lettering parked out back in the parking lot. When I was five years old, my dad moved our family from the city into a five-bedroom, split-level suburban home he built and wired himself. I heard several times growing up that the original deed for that corner half acre, dated somewhere around the 1700s, had stated that the land "must never be sold to Negros." Time and laws had long since changed, but I grew up under constant and shadowed reminders that being black was not the same as being white. In fact, my father had made the decision to move our family to the suburbs because of school desegregation laws of the 1960s which required my brothers and me to be bussed from the city to attend suburban schools. My father decided that rather than being bussed to the suburbs, we would move there.

We were the first black family in the neighborhood. I grew up splitting my time between my white neighbors and classmates in suburbs and my relatives and black friends in city. My family would drive back to the city for choir practice on Saturday afternoons, and most Saturday nights you'd find my brothers and I at the roller rink working up a sweat to the latest disco tunes. On Sunday mornings our house was a flurry of activity as my brothers polished their shoes and put on suit jackets and ties. In the kitchen my mother would set out orange juice and fresh pastries she had bought at the bakery the day before. Then she would call me into the bathroom, brush my hair, approve of the dress I selected to wear, and my family was off to church. Every single Sunday morning, without fail.

Sometimes after church, my family would stop by Porky's, a drive-in hamburger stand on University Avenue. My dad would order through a speaker and moments later a waitress in a pink uniform would emerge, carrying a red tray burgeoning with burgers, fries, and chocolate milkshakes. She'd attach the tray to the driver's side window. Dad would then pass out the grease-stained wax paper bags and each of us would get a chocolate milkshake in a brown and white-checkered paper cup. Those were the best milkshakes in the whole world. I remember there was always a solid dollop of ice cream at the bottom of the cup. My brothers and I couldn't wait to get to it. Being the only girl, I was usually seated in the front seat between my mom and dad. My four brothers were in the back seat of our green Oldsmobile 98. Once Dad had passed out the burgers, the Battles would go in. We threw down. The only sound in the car would be chewing and the crinkling of the wax paper bags and slurping as we made short of work of those chocolate milkshakes. Sometimes my dad would grab some fries from one of us, or take a slurp from one of our shakes. Sometimes he'd take a bite out of my burger and I was delighted to share. He was my hero, a big, six-foot-four, handsome man with wavy jet-black hair who worked hard to provide for his family. I didn't know it back then, but the reason why he sometimes shared our burgers and fries is because he only had enough money to buy dinner for his family and not for himself. "Got enough," he would simply say. When we were all finished he'd place the empty cups and wrappers back on the red tray and ring for the waitress to come retrieve it. He'd then roll up the window, start the engine, put the car in drive, and we'd head back to the burbs, satiated and ready for a Sunday afternoon nap.

During the week I took classical piano lessons, creative writing, and etiquette classes. My brothers worked with Dad down at the electrical shop during summer break. In the fall my brothers played football and went to Boy Scouts back in the burbs. His senior year in high school, my oldest brother, BJ, was both captain of the football team and homecoming king. I was editor of the school newspaper, worked on the yearbook committee, and got the lead role in the fall musical. Back in 1979, my high school drama teacher, whether intentionally or not, had made a statement by casting a black actress as the lead in *Hello Dolly*. The entire cast was white, except for me and my brother Nate in the chorus. My mother came to every single performance.

Even though my brothers and I often found ourselves the only black children in the room, my parents were determined to teach us life would not be limited because of the color of our skin, and that probably had a lot do with their own childhood. My father was born in Mississippi. A preacher's kid, he was just fifteen years old when he met my mother at a church convention in Memphis. He was twenty and my mother was nineteen when they married. Dad spent a few years in the army in Fort Bliss, Texas, before he and my mother moved north to join all but one of his eight brothers who had all moved to St. Paul in order to escape the Jim Crow and separate -but-equal encroachments of the South. Out of fear for their safety, my grandfather wanted all of his children to move north. Stories from that time, like the 1955 brutal murder of Mississippi teen Emmett Till, added validity to my grandfather's concerns.

My dad's oldest brother was the minister with the TV show and the pastor for whom a street in St. Paul is now named. He was the first of the family to come to St. Paul, in order to attend Bible college.

Years later, I learned it was *this* brother whom my dad brought to the hospital the night I was born to pray over me. My mom, dad, aunts, uncles, and church members all feared I wasn't going to make it and so praying was all that they could do.

Seven days later, the doctor gave my parents the all-clear to take me home.

And now here I was, three decades later, married and pregnant and about to give birth to a child of my own.

As the hours wore on, the pain increased, and then all hell broke loose. At one point I sat straight up in bed, leaned over, and threw up Popsicle juice all over the hospital room floor as my body went into convulsions. The nurses had to prop me up and hold me still me while I scribbled what would have to pass for my signature on the release form approving an epidural. It was a mad scramble to save me and my baby. My body was poisoning itself and the baby had to come out. The room filled with nurses and my OB/GYN positioned himself at the foot of my hospital bed. My husband took my hand and told me to breathe deeply, and then everyone in the room told me to push, which I did. I thought it would hurt more than it did, but I guess that's why I had signed the form for the epidural.

After a few hard pushes my son was finally born. The nurse wrapped him in a blanket and passed him over my belly so I could see him. The first time I laid eyes on my newborn baby boy, he was staring right at me; our eyes locked and the bond was instant. He laid there in my arms, eyes wide open, looking up and cooing at me. He never cried. He literally came out of the womb smiling. The doctor and nurses gathered around and marveled at how beautiful he was. I looked up at my husband and was surprised to see big, silent tears running down his cheeks as he stood looking down at his son. We had initially decided to name him Keith after his dad, but after some thought we agreed we didn't want our son growing up to be a "junior" or "the second." So we named him Jared after a name I found in a baby book and used "Keith" for his middle name.

My son and I spent the first night of his life together. He was in a bassinet beside me. The nurses were a little upset with me because I refused to put Jared in the nursery overnight; they kept insisting that I needed to rest, but there was no part of me that wanted to be separated from this beautiful tiny life I had just been introduced to. He was staying with me, in my room, period.

Keith had stayed as long as he could tolerate the small pull-out bed before leaving, exhausted, to get a good night's rest at home. Jared woke up every few hours that night making tiny little sounds, sort of cross between a chirp and a coo and a whimper. The nurses had showed me how to breastfeed, so I would feed him, change his tiny diaper if needed, and then wrap him tight in his blanket before putting him back to sleep in the bassinet.

The next morning Keith returned, rested, and sat with his son while I went to bathe and change clothes. I will never forget what the doctor said to me just as we were being released to go home. His name was Dr. Goldfarb, and he was an older Jewish gentleman with large hands and kind eyes. He examined Jared before our release and I stood there watching with tears running down my face. I had never loved anything as much as I loved my son. I apologized for crying so much and Dr. Goldfarb reassured that it was normal with new moms and caused by all those pregnancy hormones still coursing through my body. Then he looked down at Jared and said, "He is the most important thing right now, not TV." I would have taken offense if I hadn't been in total agreement. It was as if God had spoken because that is exactly how I felt at that very moment. Little did I know then how those words would circle back around in the years to come.

2

FLYING SOLO

Now to Him who is able to do exceedingly abundantly above all
that we ask or think, according to the power that works in us.
—Ephesians 3:20

My son was just eleven months old when my marriage ended.

In three short years, I had gone from newlywed to new mom to divorced single mom with an infant. My ex-husband and I had taken a year and a half to build the house we were living in. After the divorce, we sold it and went our separate ways. I was granted sole physical custody of my son, and the two of us moved into a small two-bedroom apartment. I signed a six-month lease but stayed in that apartment five years. I had moved in during the heat of the summer, and now, months later, winter's chill had crept in.

I was a new mom, with a new baby, a divorce decree, and a reporter job on the five o'clock news. I remember one evening I stood at my bedroom window, watching white flakes fall silently from the sky, dancing around pools of amber light cast by the evening street lights, and hoping that the season's change signaled not just the passing of time but also a distancing from pain. *Maybe this sadness and depression will pass too*, I thought.

Every week, it seemed, brought new adjustments and difficult moments. I had to learn to hand my baby off and see him buckled in and driven away into the darkness for visitations with his dad. As Jared grew, so did his bond with his father, to the point where visitation became an unnecessary formality. What started out as a few days a week stretched into weekends and even weeks at a time. The two of them would often take long trips out of town over holiday breaks. While I was thankful for my son's developing relationship with his father, the discord from our split still resonated in the early days as we struggled to coexist. My ex-husband would come to Saturday afternoon parks and rec basketball games, but we would sit apart from each other in the bleachers. The fact that we weren't together was obvious, awkward, and always required an explanation. I found myself having to spell out over and over during parent-teacher conferences why I was attending alone. I understand why God hates divorce. So do I. Day in, day out, I was now flying solo.

And yet, I created my own routine for my little family. Every day, I'd get up, get dressed, get my son dressed, feed him breakfast, and then drop him off at the child care center across the street from my apartment, kiss his plump caramel-colored cheek, and watch as the curly-haired, brown-eyed love of my life bounded off into the toddler room before I headed into work at the television station. At the end of the day, I'd pick him up, sometimes make a stop at the grocery store, and then head home to make dinner, take baths, read stories, say prayers, tuck him into bed, and do it all over again the next day.

I didn't know it then, but looking back I can see now how these routines were more like rituals, and how important they were. Like most kids, Jared loved bath time. He always wanted lots of bubbles, and while I ran the bathwater he would toss his bath toys in the tub one at time, giggling as they made tiny splashes in water. His favorite bath toy was a small blue plastic whale he mistakenly named "Mr. Beaver." Eric Carle's *The Very Hungry Caterpillar* and *The Very Busy Spider* were always at the foot of the bed. He also loved the rhyming and the rhythm of *God Made Me So I Must Be Special*. I bought the African-American version, and as I read, he'd look and smile at the little brown faces on each page. Faces that looked like him. But our favorite was *Love You Forever*. Jared absolutely loved this one. "Again," he would say when I reached the end, and I'd start it all over again from the beginning.

We'd sit there in bed for the better part of an hour every night, me reading book after book to the delight of my curious little boy.

Then, finally prayers. Jared would lead off and I'd repeat:

"Dear God, bless Mommy. Bless Daddy. Bless Jared. Thank You for everything that is good and right in the world. Amen."

I'd pull back the covers and he'd crawl underneath. And then in a whisper I'd make him the same promise made in *Love You Forever*:

I'll love you forever
I'll like you for always
As long as I'm living
My baby you'll be. [1]

I'd kiss his forehead, and with those big, brown, and now-sleepy eyes looking up at me, I'd say, "Love you, JJ." He'd say, "Love you, Mommy," and, content, he'd roll over on his side and off to sleep.

There was this one bedtime when, because of Jared's precocious little mind, I didn't know whether to laugh or cry. We were reading a book on farm animals. I'd read to him about the mama sheep and the mama cow and the mama ducks when he interrupted me and pointed to an illustration of baby pigs suckling. He asked me what the pigs were doing so I explained that the baby pigs were hungry and the mommy pig was feeding them. He asked what the piggies were eating. I said the mama piggy's nipples were giving the baby piggies milk. He seemed satisfied with my explanation and we continued with the story. When it came time for prayers, just as always, at the edge of the bed on our knees, side by side, hands clasped, heads bowed, Jared began and I repeated:

38

"Dear God,"
"Dear God,"
"Bless Mommy,"
"Bless Mommy,"
"Bless Daddy,"
"Bless Daddy,"
"Bless Jared,"
"Bless Jared,"

Then, this little boy of mine, who was no more than two years old, finished, "And bless the piggy's nipples."

I fell out across the bed howling with laughter. I just cracked up. I buried my face in the blankets and laughed and laughed. I glanced over at my son to find him impishly giggling away. He seemed to take great pleasure in the fact he had made his mommy laugh.

"You little stinker, get in the bed!" I said, still laughing.

He hopped under the covers, giggling and wiggling in a pair of long-sleeved Power Rangers pajamas.

Little stinker, I thought as I turned off the light. *Making mama laugh.* I'm reminded of a Bible verse that says, *"Weeping may endure for a night, but joy comes in the morning."*[2] Thanks to my precocious little PJ-clad kid, I didn't have to wait until the morning; I had a pocket of joy that night.

Gosh, how precious those days were. With everything in my adult world falling apart and me working so hard to put it all back together again, how precious it was to be able to end each day, however hectic, with this little ritual, this little pocket. No matter the tumult in my adult world, my "little man," as I called him sometimes, went to bed feeling safe, cared for, and loved. Despite everything that had gone wrong, at least this seemed to be something that was going right. And that was enough for me to get up and try again and look for the joy the next day as I dropped off my boy and headed to work.

I look back on that time and see how people must have thought I lived such a glamorous life—on TV, meeting celebrities, and going on fascinating adventures and assignments. One of my best stories is the time I flew out to L.A. and got sick as a dog in the back of a cab on my way to Burbank. I was there to do a piece on a Minnesota grade-schooler who had been invited to do a guest spot on *The Tonight Show* with Jay Leno. The little girl had made thousands of bracelets out of hemp and red clay hearts and was sending the bracelets to soldiers on deployment in Iraq. We had run the story locally and *The Tonight Show* called, saying Jay thought the hemp angle was "interesting." Traffic en route to *The Tonight Show* studios was ridiculous and typical for L.A.—stop and go on the 405 and for much of the two-hour ride from the airport. By the time I got to Burbank, I was laid out flat in the backseat with a really bad case of motion sickness.

40 As I crawled out of the cab, Mr. Leno's producer met me and said if I wanted an interview with Jay I'd better hustle because he was about to tape the show and my only shot of getting a one-on-one with him was right then. Into the building, past security, and down a narrow hall, I could hear *The Tonight Show* band warming up. The little girl, her family, and Deb, a cameraperson from the station, had caught an earlier flight, and I caught up with Deb as she was interviewing the girl and her mother in the greenroom backstage.

I hadn't been in the building five minutes; I was woozy, my stomach was gurgling, and there, coming down the hall directly toward me, was Jay Leno. Deb spotted him and quickly grabbed the camera off the tripod, hoisted it onto her shoulder, and handed me a microphone. Bam, I was on, bright light in my face and five minutes with *Tonight Show* host Jay Leno, who in person was shorter than I had imagined. He was gracious and funny and joked on camera about alternative uses for hemp. He answered the last of my three questions, then, satisfied that I had gotten what I needed, he thanked me for coming out to L.A. and turned and walked back down the hall onto *The Tonight Show* set, and that was it. Arnold Schwarzenegger was also on the show that night, dressed in a crisp white button-down shirt and navy blue sport coat. I was impressed with how good he looked in person and how he had intentionally greeted everyone in the greenroom, including me, with a nod and a smile before leaving with a small entourage.

However, those types of gee-whiz reporting gigs happened only every so often. The truth of the matter was, away from the camera, my life was ordinary and, at times, it seemed to me, extraordinarily lonely and sad. I was living on a starting reporter's salary, which didn't come close to the six-figure incomes the station's main anchors were making. My child support payments came without fail, but still, I was broke. There was rent and utilities, the daycare and car payment, plus thousands of dollars in divorce-attorney fees that still had to be paid. And contrary to what the public may have believed, the station did not pay for my clothes or hair appointments.

One night at dinner, when Jared was about two-and-a-half years old, it all came down to a chicken nugget and a handful of French fries. I was between paydays, and I only had enough money to buy my little boy a Happy Meal. I sat and watched as his little fingers picked up a nugget and brought it to his mouth. Next, one by one, he ate some fries, then another nugget. I was just grateful that at least one of us had dinner. After a bit, he said he was done. I picked

41

him up and sat him in front of the TV and put in a video, then went back to the dinner table. There, on his plate, was one leftover nugget and a few fries. My dinner. Who would have thought a Happy Meal could produce a nugget-size pocket of joy? To this day, I still wonder if my little boy had left that nugget on purpose, because he knew his mommy was hungry. I guess I'll never know.

It seemed that without even trying, my son had a way of making me smile. One night a few years later, after we had moved out of the apartment and into a small home of our own, I was exhausted after a very long and hard day.

42   It was early March, and instead of the usual rain that cleared the ground of winter's remnants, six inches of snow had fallen. The station had positioned me alongside Interstate 394 to warn viewers of the evening commute. Backups and traffic accidents. I knew more about plow trucks and road solvents than I really cared to. If I had done one hazardous winter-driving live shot, I had done dozens of them.

Now, the workday was over and I was stuck in the very traffic I had just warned viewers to avoid. By March, winter makes one weary. Traffic is slower, and everyone, including the heartiest Midwesterner, is so ready for it to be over. All I wanted was to crawl into bed and sleep.

But I still needed groceries. Friday nights were always pizza nights, so, thankfully, dinner would be easy. As the constant wickety-whack of my windshield wipers played on, I fought through the snow and "slow-and-go" traffic to my son's grade school. By now he had grown into a bright-eyed and delightfully precocious third-grader. Once he was signed out and buckled in, we headed to the grocery store.

Bread, milk, eggs, the usual. Except he wanted a cookie.

"Mom, can I have some cookies with the green sprinkles on them?"

"Sure."

We stopped by the bakery. We didn't see any in the case so we asked the lady behind the counter if she had any sugar cookies with green sprinkles. After all, Saint Patrick's Day was right around the corner.

43

"How many would you like?" she asked.

"Three." One for after dinner, another for Saturday, and one more to pack in his lunch on Monday.

"I'll be right back," she said before disappearing behind two swinging metal doors. Moments later she returned with a white waxed paper bag, and inside were his three cookies. "There you are," she said, smiling as she handed the bag to Jared.

And just as I was about to remind him, he said, "Thank you."

Content, we continued to shop. Bananas, strawberries, juice boxes. On to the frozen-food aisle.

"What kind of pizza do you want," I asked him. "DiGiorno or Tombstone?"

"Eenie, meenie, miny, moe…."

Oh Lord, I thought. *I just don't have the patience for this.*

"If he hollers, let him go…." He had an audience now. I was just waiting for someone on the overhead to announce cart backup in frozen foods.

"I. Want. The. Ver-ree. Best. One." DiGiorno it was. Pepperoni. I bought two, to avoid having to go through this again the next week.

Lunch meat, ground turkey, spaghetti sauce, noodles. That was going to have to do it. I was wiped out. Now the wait in the checkout line.

"Mom, can I eat one of my cookies?"

No surprise there. Shoulda had more resolve. Sweets before dinner? In what how-to parenting guide has that ever been mentioned as appropriate?

"You sure it won't spoil your appetite?"

"I'm sure."

It had been a long day, and he hadn't eaten since lunch. What the heck.

"Whatever."

He sat on a bench between the ATM and the ice freezer, eating his cookie while the checkout clerk rang up and bagged our groceries. *What did I buy?* I thought as I swiped my cash card for $139. Approved.

We headed for the parking lot, cookie crumbs all over his mouth. I was whipped, just beat, and I still had to drive through snow in the cold car and unload all those groceries, then put the pizza in the oven for his dinner. Clean out the fridge. Unload the dishwasher; probably should put in a load of laundry. *Wonder if his basketball shorts are clean for his game tomorrow?*

"Hey, Mom."

He had been sitting quietly in the front seat playing his Game Boy. Some game called *Supersonic*.

"Yeah, buddy?"

"You're fun to love," he said, glancing up quickly and flashing a grin.

I wanted to make sure I heard what I thought I heard.

"Excuse me?"

"You're fun to love…you're cool to love. I just love you, Mommy."

Stunned really wasn't the word. *Teary-eyed* or *delighted* was better.

"That's really nice, Jared. I love you, too."

He was quiet again. I continued driving. I guess he had been deep in thought too, only it wasn't an exhaustive list of chores he had been thinking about.

"You're a loaf."

"Huh?"

"You're a loaf, Mom," he said without looking up. "You're my lovable loaf."

OK, so blame it on the cookie. Was my son so sweet and sugary before dinner because I let him have sweets and sugar before dinner? Maybe. Or maybe, just maybe, this spontaneous expression of love had to do with something else: routine. Maybe something as mundane as going to the grocery store together allowed him to feel secure enough to call me a…loaf.

Either that, or we had spent way more time than I realized in the bread aisle.

Years later, when I told Jared the "lovable loaf" story, he told me that at the time he was mimicking his favorite cartoon character, Double Dee, from *Ed, Edd n Eddy*, except in hindsight he realized that instead of "lovable loaf," Double Dee's signature line was actually "lovable oaf."

Even though I loved being a mom, I struggled for years adjusting to the reality of being the head of household, single parent, and breadwinner.

One evening, I got a call from a former news director, now working at a station in another city. She was calling to offer me the main anchor job at her station. She made me the offer and asked for my decision. I told her I needed some time to think about it. She said she wanted to fill the position right away and needed an answer in twenty-four hours.

Here was the opportunity I had been working for my entire career! I would be the main anchor of the five, six, and eleven o'clock news. I imagined my face on billboards around town and on the sides of busses. No one would be able to argue whether I was a success—not to mention the boost in pay. How I needed the money! It seemed like a great opportunity.

But then I realized that the new job would mean taking my son far away from his dad. The two of them were beginning to form a real, loving relationship, and I was torn. On top of that, if I took the job and moved away, who would look after my son while I was working late at night? I wouldn't be getting home during the week until midnight. Sure, I could hire a nanny, but that would cut into the new salary I'd be making. I realized that I certainly could fly my son back to Minnesota to see his father, but even if we split the airfare, it would still cut into the new salary. I did the math and figured out what it would cost in airplane tickets to have my son maintain a relationship with his father, and what it would cost to have someone look after him late at night five days a week while I was working the eleven o'clock news. In the end I decided it just wasn't worth it. Call me crazy, but I called the news director back and told her no. I turned the job down.

The opportunity to become a main weekday news anchor never came again. The wave had passed. In hindsight, that decision was probably one of the biggest sacrifices I've made in my life. If it had just been me, I would have taken the job. But I was a single mom with a young child to think about, and I had a goal: to do the best job I could raising him. To me that meant even though I needed the money, my son needed his father more, and so I stayed in Minneapolis and continued working as a general-assignment news reporter.

It was a sacrifice that could have very well cost me my career. My colleagues were stunned that I turned the anchor job down. They began to question whether I was serious about my career. Wasn't a main anchor gig everything I had been working toward? In many ways, yes, but for whatever reason, something inside compelled me to put my tiny little family—me and my boy—ahead of my career.

A few years later, the station promoted me to weekend anchor. It wasn't the main anchor job, but the raise I got with the new position here in my hometown was the same as the salary the out-of-town news director had offered me to leave. So I was making the same money but without having to move to a new city. I was an anchor. My boy was near his dad. All the things I had prayed for, believed in, made sacrifices and unpopular decisions for, happened. For whatever reason, God had smiled on me. Just when I thought my career was toast, I got the opportunity that I thought had eluded me, right here in my hometown.

I tucked the additional income away into a savings account until I had enough money to make a down payment on a small three-bedroom house. My goal was to move out of the apartment I was renting by the time my son started kindergarten.

It took me three and half years, but I closed on our new home in the fall of my son's kindergarten year. It took a lot of sacrifice, but the day we walked into our house made it all worth it. I was a homeowner, and our new home was fifteen minutes from my son's school, ten minutes from my job, and surrounded by great neighbors. They helped me with everything. There was Elizabeth, who helped me plant my small garden. We'd spend sunny Saturday afternoons talking about hostas and New Guinea impatiens while her black-and-white cat, Micah, whom Jared loved, roamed the yard. Mr. Johnson from across the driveway would fix my plumbing and hammer holes in my walls so I could hang pictures. His wife, Diane, made the best homemade chocolate-chip cookies, hands down. She wasn't always feeling well, so she'd send Mr. Johnson over with a brown paper bag of warm cookies. There was my neighbor Jean, a retired schoolteacher who taught piano lessons. Her grandchildren would always come visit, and whenever I was out on the deck grilling, Jean would tease me about inviting the entire neighborhood over for a barbeque.

I loved that tiny house. I painted the kitchen raspberry pink and bought a new sofa for the living room. I stayed up until 2:00 a.m. painting over the peach seashells and aqua seahorses in my son's room, left from the previous owners, and replacing them with bright yellow paint and basketball borders. I hung curtains and bought him a matching bed set and a toy box shaped like a basketball. This was the place we would call home for the next eight years.

One of our first Thanksgivings in our home, I was in the kitchen making a peach cobbler that my family always requested I bring over to dinner at my parent's home. Jared was parked in front of the television watching the Macy's Thanksgiving Day Parade, when suddenly he came running into the kitchen in a panic.

"Mom, Mom! There's naked ladies on TV!"

"What, Jared?"

"Yeah, Mom, the man said there are gonna be naked ladies on TV!" He was wide-eyed with anxiety and quite alarmed at the possibility.

"Jared," I said calmly. "There are not going to be any naked ladies on TV, and there are certainly not any naked ladies at the Macys' Thanksgiving Day Parade."

"Uh-huh Mom! Yes there is! He said so!"

"Who said so, Jared?"

"The man. He said so, Mom!"

"Jared, what did the man say?"

"He said, coming up next, naked ladies!"

I realized Jared was referring to the television announcer who would announce what floats and musical acts would be coming up after the commercial break. So I said to Jared, "Okay, son, let's go see what this is all about."

We went and sat on the couch in the living room and waited for the parade to come back on after the commercial break. Then sure enough, the announcer said:

"And now, singing 'Auld Lang Syne,' from their new holiday album, here are the Barenaked Ladies!"

"See Mom? See? Bare naked ladies are on TV! See, I told you!"

Oh my. My little guy had really worked himself up about this. Ever since he was very young, Jared had a thing against scantily-clad women on TV. Even before he could pronounce his l's properly, he would constantly yell at the screen for them to "put some cwothes on."

"Jared, honey," I explained, "look at the TV. See there, the Barenaked Ladies is a band. That's the name of a band. A musical group. There are no naked ladies on TV."

He stood there, blank faced, looking at the TV for few seconds and then blurted, "Well, that's stupid! Who names a band 'Barenaked Ladies'?"

"You good son? I gotta go finish making my pie."

51

"That is so dumb, Mom! Who does that?!"

I still laugh about it to this day.

3

LITTLE FABIO

No temptation has overtaken you except such as is common to
*man, but God is faithful, who **will not allow you to be tempted***
***beyond what you are able,** but with the temptation will also*
make the way of escape, that you may be able to bear it.
—1 Corinthians 10:13

52   A few months before my fortieth birthday, I flew to Cancun,
Mexico, alone. It was the week before Christmas; I had been
divorced for several years now, was still single, and my son was
spending the holiday with his dad. It was the dead of winter in
Minnesota, with piles of snow on the ground and brutally cold
windchills in the air, making it the perfect time to escape to trop-
ical weather. Knowing I would be spending Christmas alone, an
attorney friend and his wife had invited me to join them for their
annual family trip to a ranch they owned on the Yucatán Peninsula.
They would be there through Christmas. I agreed to join them for
a few days before flying home to have Christmas with my parents.

Up until now, my attempts at dating as a single divorcée had
ranged from boring to disastrous. For me, dating was like Ben

Gay: something you rub on to take the pain away…for a little a while.

It stinks.

And it's messy.

And eventually, the pain comes right back.

For quite a while I thought I was the reigning queen of first dates. Not because the dates went well, but rather because more often than not they didn't.

"I don't find you TV people all that interesting," one guy said over a plate of bruschetta appetizers.

Then why am I here?

53

I was just praying I'd make it to the main course. It always seemed they put their foot rather than their fork in their mouths minutes after the bread basket and pats of butter arrived. Which left me to suffer through the main course, and them to wonder days and weeks later why I had no interest in a followup.

Then there was the lunch date. *Lunch,* I thought, *is safe. No time to linger…short and sweet, in and out, nobody gets hurt. Right?* Wrong.

"I think your show is boring."

Okay. Fine. You're certainly entitled to that opinion, but why you would want to share that so soon after exchanging the obligatory first-date niceties, is beyond me.

At least we had made it through the salad with bleu cheese dressing and croutons.

Then there was the all-time date from hell. We were going to dinner and a movie. The tip-off should have been when he asked me to pick him up. Which I did. Mistake number one. I had met him at a concert a few weeks before and we had chatted briefly and exchanged numbers during intermission. There had been a few brief telephone calls. He seemed pleasant. So when he finally got around to asking me out, I agreed. How far perception differs from reality.

For starters, he needed a bath. Badly. A fact I am certain he was aware of, since as he buckled himself into the passenger seat it became immediately apparent that he had deemed cologne, not soap, to be the appropriate remedy. But being the then-so-needy person that I was, I thought, *I just picked him up from work. I mean, he would have bathed if he hadn't been so eager to see me, right?*

We headed to the Mall of America and up to a sports bar on the fourth floor.

We ordered appetizers because that's all he said he was hungry for. Tip-off number two. I, on the other hand, could have eaten a small pony.

I ordered a Sprite. He ordered Jack Daniels. Straight. Strike three. We sat there sucking on hot buffalo wings and stuffed potato wedges trying to make small talk. When the bill came, he reached inside his pocket and pulled out a crumpled mess of dollar bills. He examined them for a moment and then asked, "You got six dollars?"

You-have-got-to-be-kidding. I gave him ten. Mistake number...I've lost track.

He had managed to produce two free movie passes. I knew popcorn was not even an option. We headed to the movie theater and saw the absolute worst movie known to mankind. Not even Lawrence Fishburne could save *Event Horizon*, a combination of Freddy Kruger meets Star Trek. People starting walking out after the first fifteen minutes. I was actually relieved because I knew it wouldn't be long before we bailed as well, thus delivering me from the overwhelming stench that comes from sitting in such close proximity to someone who so desperately needed to bathe. And yes, he had draped his arm over the back of my chair.

Back in the car, we were driving back to his workplace, presumably to get his car, when his cell phone rang.

"Hello...oh hey, honey."

Honey?

"Yeah...uh, let me call you back. Yeah. Bye."

Not that during our brief, yet insufferable time together had I come even remotely close to developing any sort of attachment or anything, but being as he was sitting in *my* car, I felt I had a right to know who "honey" was. And given the way the evening had gone up unto this point, why should I have been surprised when he said "honey" was his wife?

"Get out."

"What?"

55

"Get out of my car...now." Politeness really was no longer required. All I could think about was attacking the passenger seat with a shammy cloth and Armor All.

"Don't I get a kiss?"

Unbe-leev-able! This man was certifiably crazy. My nerves had been severely tested and frayed, and all I wanted to was to be rid of him. And so in the most calm and controlled voice I could muster I said;

"Get-your-funky-behind-out-of-my-car, now."

"Dang, baby. Can I call you?"

"GET OUT!"

56

Yeah. That all happened one summer. I wanted to kick myself for going out with such a loser. Was I so lonely, so desperate that I had overlooked obvious red flags? Was I so afraid of being alone that I was willing to sublimate—to make excuses just to keep myself from feeling lonely?

Honestly, the answer was yes.

I did some soul-searching after what can only be described as the date from hell. I realized if I was ever going to truly heal from the divorce, I had to stop putting myself in compromising situations and stop looking for my happiness in someone else. I had to learn to be happy, all by myself. Within myself.

That's a lot easier said than done, especially when you're feeling tired and stressed out. Especially when you feel like all you do is get up every day and grind it out. Work, home, my son, dinner, and bedtime, with little time for me. I had to get a grip. I had to find a way to get in touch with myself. I felt I had to learn how to be content, alone. Yes, maybe someday there would again be someone special in my life, but what was I going to do in the meantime? Spend the here and now feeling sorry for myself and obsessing about what I'd lost, worrying about what's to come? Or maybe, just maybe, I could choose to spend the here and now *being* in the here and now. Being aware of today and not wishing for it to be anything more than what it is. I think I was slowly beginning to realize that life was not one big rom-com where the guy gets the girl and they kiss in the park and run off blissfully into never-never land. I was beginning to see that being coupled up with someone was not the only definition of happiness.

So rather than spending my energies looking for my proverbial knight in shining armor, I started looking for joy wherever it might be found. Instead of feeling left out on Valentine's Day, for example, my son and I would sit at our dining room table the night before and cut out valentines and Scotch-tape heart-shaped suckers to each one, which Jared would sign for his classmates and bring to school the next day. Some years I'd even bake heart-shaped sugar cookies and Jared would help me frost them. We did this all throughout his grade school years and it brought me great joy being able to spend this one-on-one time with him and see his excitement about passing out treats to his friends at school.

I bought a set of golf clubs, took golf lessons, and joined the women's golf league at work. Every Wednesday while Jared was with his dad or with a sitter, I'd play nine holes with my coworkers at the golf course across the street from the television station. Sometimes we'd find golf balls in the grass by the station parking lot, the result of an overly ambitious golfer whose not-so-accurate swing had driven a ball over the fence. I actually fell in love with golfing. I loved the scenery and solitude, walking the course on a warm, muggy summer night, and finishing up the last hole just before sunset. Whenever I'd drain a putt or shoot par, one of my regular golf buddies would always remark, "Now that, Roxane, was a thing of beauty." As I got better at the game, golfing became great fun. I played in other women's leagues and all kinds of charity golf tournaments. I even won a trophy or two! One year I met the great Michael Jordan when he came to town to play in a charity golf event. Aside from the celebs and trophies, it was always so peaceful out on the course. Sometimes I'd see a deer or a bunny rabbit or stop briefly to listen to a babbling creek while fishing my ball out of the rough. I'd admire the landscaping and flowers and on really long holes it seemed like I could see forever. Being out on a golf course was the only time I truly forgot about being on television or my responsibilities at home. Once I picked up the game, I never stopped playing. I had found one of my happy places.

There were also church conferences and women's meetings, coffee and lunches with my girlfriends that occupied what free time I had and kept me from feeling so alone. And yes, of course, there was shopping. I was a bargain hunter's bargain hunter. I loved shoes and porcelain teacups and would scour discount stores to add to my growing collection of both.

I had done all of this on purpose. I had intentionally gone out into the world looking for joy. And yes, from time to time I found it. Most of the time it didn't come wrapped up in a bow or packed in a heart-shaped box. Most of time it was the simple things: sunlight, the smell of wet dirt as I watered my garden, fresh cut grass, and solitude. Time to think and reflect about where I've been, where I am now and how all of that was going to help me get to where I wanted to be: happy.

The flight to Mexico was less than half full. There were so few passengers that most of us stretched out across an entire row of seats and napped during the long flight. I thought that strange, since Minnesotans are notorious snowbirds, known for escaping to warm-weather retreats during the long winter. I also thought this whole trip was a little strange. I mean, who owns a *ranch* on the Yucatán Peninsula? I was grateful for the invitation, but at the same time didn't want to intrude on what seemed like a family tradition. That's why I decided to fly down early and spend four days by myself in Playa del Carmen on the Riviera Maya.

Turning forty as a single made me feel a little sorry for myself. I had read somewhere that the odds of a woman over forty getting married again were about the same as being struck by lightning. But rather than be overwhelmed and depressed by my later-in-life single status, I decided to focus on what was *right* in my life. I was in good health. I had a good job. My son was healthy and thriving. I had bought a small home and, by all accounts, my life was settling and stabilizing, even if I was doing it all alone. I decided to take this trip as a marker. I was going to, once and for all, put away the hurt of the past and focus on the future, and turning forty was the perfect time to celebrate all that was right in my life thus far.

My attorney friends had helped me book a small room right on the waterfront. The ocean waves were just a few paces from my sliding glass door. Inside, however, the accommodations were stark and minimalist to say the least: stone floors; a dark-brown wooden table with four chairs; a mint-green, cotton-covered pull-out sofa that had been slept on, crashed on, done-whatever-on one time too many; and a queen-size bed with just a thin cotton sheet for a spread. "Bohemian and quaint" was how my friends had described the hotel. They said I'd love it. Whatever. I was on the beach and far away from home, ready to start over.

In my suitcase, along with flip-flops, T-shirts, and shorts, was a hot pink bikini. I hadn't worn a bikini since I was twelve years old, when there was far less for so little to cover. Whenever I was at the pool with my son, I had always worn a very conservative one-piece, which I had also packed. In fact, even professionally I was quite a conservative dresser at the time. Flat shoes, boxy jackets, and straight skirts were wardrobe staples for me.

But for now, here on the beach with the warm Yucatán sun bearing down, a bikini was all about being a woman—not a mom, but a woman. Getting in touch with that part of myself. I wasn't brave enough to wear it without covering up, so I put on a pair of white shorts before I stepped out of my room onto the beach. What did I expect? I don't know. Odd looks? A gasp? A stare? Truth is, no one noticed. They were all too busy trying very hard not to look at the very tan and very thin older couple walking hand in hand along the beach in matching lime-green thongs and nothing else.

Dear Lord! Quite the shocker for this Midwestern conservative Christian girl! This was the Riviera Maya. No one cared about my corny, hot pink bikini top. No one on the beach was even *wearing* a top! I laughed at myself and my naïveté. This was going to be an interesting trip.

Every morning, I'd put on a pair of shorts and a T-shirt, grab my flip-flops, and walk up the beach to the pier. There I'd buy fresh papaya, pineapple, and coconut for five pesos. The local women would come early in the morning in their crisp white ruffled blouses and colorful skirts, their long black hair tied up in pretty buns. They'd make makeshift tables out of a few slabs of wood and large rocks. I'd watch as they methodically dove into whole pieces of fruit with very large knives, chopping and dicing and scooping fruit pieces into plastic cups ready for sale.

Then, I'd just sit on the beach and listen to the waves. Sometimes I'd ride the ferry over to Cancun and sit at an open-air restaurant, order tacos, and people-watch, which was a lot of fun, especially on the days a cruise ship would dock. I'd watch as tourists from the ship spilled onto the beach for a shore excursion, fanny packs, digital cameras, and sunscreen in tow.

My last day there, I went snorkeling with a group of tourists. Our snorkeling guide looked every bit like the Italian

61

fashion model Fabio, only younger, like he could have been his little brother. He was wearing pale-blue swim shorts and nothing else, his long blond hair trailing down his bare back in loose waves, his body perfectly toned and tanned.

Over the last few days, I had observed Little Fabio's mode of operation. In the morning, he would cruise up and down the beach on foot, looking for customers who fit one of two criteria: couples that were on a shore visit, and lonely unattached women, like me.

"Good morning," he said.

I hadn't seen him approach. I had been sitting at a table on the beach at an open-air restaurant, my feet in the sand, listening to the waves a few feet away, drinking the last of my orange juice.

"Good morning!" I could see his intent was to startle me.

"Are choo alone?"

"Yes." *Why did I say that?!*

"May I sit down?"

"Sure." *Oh my, was this an "adventure"?*

He began to tell me about his boat, the *Bunny Bunny*. Only with his Mexican accent it sounded like *Bonny, Bonny*. He named it after his bunny, his pet rabbit, which had died. He went on about some cruise-ship passengers who had stiffed him after his last snorkeling excursion.

"Can choo imageen!"

He was charming and funny, and no more than twenty years old, if that. I was flattered to have caught his attention, pushing forty and all, and I began to wonder if he wanted a customer, a date, or both.

"Do choo have plans this morning?" he asked.

"No, not really."

"Would choo like to go snorkeling?"

"When?"

"Right now."

"Now!"

"Ches, now."

"How much?"

"Twenty dohlers."

"Twenty…that's all?"

"Ches. I will take choo personally and show you the leetle tiny blue fish. Choo like coral? I will show choo the coral. Ches?"

"Yes." *What was I doing?!*

I ran back to my hotel room, changed into that conservative one-piece swimsuit, and moments later I was on the *Bonny Bonny*—uh, *Bunny Bunny*—a motorboat speeding away from the hotel on the open water with six other tourists and Little Fabio.

Are you crazy? I thought. *You could die out here!*

But I was sucked in by the spontaneity and sense of adventure. I did see those little tiny blue fish, and coral. Little Fabio made good on his promise to give me a personalized tour of the ocean bottom. I got lost in the underwater world, the blues and greens and the glint of the sun on the water. I forgot how far away from home I was, or that the snorkeling equipment smelled like Clorox bleach. I could hear myself breathing through the snorkel tube and felt the ocean water washing over me. The fish, the water, the sun. I was free.

When the *Bunny Bunny* got back to the hotel beachfront, I hopped off with the rest of the tourists and one by one, we each handed Little Fabio a damp twenty-dollar bill. I then headed to my room for a shower and a nap, alone.

64 That night I sat on the beach and had dinner by myself. Storm clouds had rolled in and lingered most of that afternoon, but by nightfall they had cleared to reveal a blue-black sky and stars that shown like jewels. I ordered a cup of seafood Pernod. It was like a fish soup, or stew, in a tomato base with lots of vegetables. My Spanish was elementary at best, but I was told the locals appreciated if you at least attempted a few words, which was something the young waiter seemed accustomed to. The soup was so good, and I wanted more.

"Otre, por favor? Otre?"

"Sí senorita, un momento."

While I waited for the second cup of soup, with my toes in the sand, watching the night sky and hearing the gentle waves on the shore, I felt a warmth creep through my limbs. I thought back to that morning, how I had let the waves of water flow over me as I scanned the ocean floor for a glimpse of what was beneath. I thought about the heat of the Yucatán sun, the softness of the white sand under my bare feet. I thought about my nap on that thin cotton sheet.

And then, there on that beach, under a blue-black sky, one by one, a thousand tiny knots released. I let go. The past was over. The hurt. The disappointment. I just let it go. It was time. I was free. Free to make new memories, to start over, to live and to dream.

"Señorita," he said as he gently set the cup of soup on my table.

"Gracias."

"De nada."

I ate the soup and ordered grilled grouper and steamed vegetables. I sat there on that beach all by myself, feasting. It was Thursday. My friends would be arriving the next morning, and by the weekend the beach and hotel would be jumping with holiday travelers. The empty stools at the outdoor bar would be filled. There would be music and dancing and all the things that come with long days in the sun and even longer nights under the stars. But for the night the beach was quiet, and I was at peace.

I was tired of being defined by what I had gone through and what I had lost. I had taken this trip as a way of freeing myself and redefining the rest of my life. It was about breaking free of fear and feeling free to live, something I hadn't felt in a very long time.

I was always worried about having enough money, my job, my career, trying to be the responsible parent, meeting my son's needs.

In some ways I had lived so much for my son, I had lost touch with myself.

So here I was in Mexico, a few months before my fortieth birthday, ready to let go of the past, celebrate the present, and move toward the future.

After dinner I walked back to the hotel, and there waiting in front of my door was Little Fabio. This time he wasn't looking for a customer.

"Choo are still alone?" he said in tone that was every bit a leading question.

"Yes...but, um...my friends will be here soon."

Uh, seriously? Is he, like, looking to, like, hook up? Earlier that day on the snorkeling excursion he had given the cute little blonde girl in a bikini lots of attention. She had actually lingered by the *Bunny Bunny* after the rest of us had left. There wasn't much doubt in my mind that the two of them had, uh, connected at some point before her cruise ship pulled out of port. Surely now he wasn't coming after me!

"Friends?" he asked, emphasizing the *s*.

"Yes...friends." I answered without further explanation.

It would have been so easy, too easy, to invite him into my room. All I had to do was literally open the door. The beach was dark and empty with only the sound of the waves. No one would have ever known except me. And God. Standing right there, in front of my hotel room, with the key in my hand, looking at his young, perfect physique, sun-bleached hair, and golden tan, I thought, *I could…but I just can't.*

I was free. I had taken this trip to let go of past hurts and start fresh, so why would I sully this experience by sleeping with a stranger? Little Fabio of all people.

"I don't see no friends," he said.

"They'll be here…soon," I said, as I inserted the key and walked into my hotel room, shutting the door behind me, amused by the fact that Little Fabio may never have realized I was old enough to be his mother.

4

PRIME TIME

You will make you prayer to Him, He will hear you, and you will pay your vows. You will also declare a thing, and it will be established for you; so light will shine on your ways. When they cast you down, and you say, "Exaltation will come!" Then He will save the humble person.
—Job 22:27–29

I had gone to church all of my life, but now that I was anchoring the weekend news, church was all but impossible. It made for a very long day to go to church on Sunday morning and anchor the 10:00 p.m. news that night. However, I began to really miss that spiritual connection. I felt I was afloat, and I really didn't want to raise my son without a godly influence in his life. When the opportunity came to shift my work schedule from weekend nights to weekday mornings, I took it. The midmorning time slot wasn't prime time; ratings at that time of day weren't as high as in the evening; and the new job was hosting a lifestyle show instead of anchoring a hard-hitting evening newscast. In other words, the midmorning show didn't carry the status or prestige of the weekend evening news, but I took the job anyway because it allowed me to take my son to church on Sundays. I could also go to his games and swimming lessons on Saturdays. I could now work a nine-to-five-thirty, Monday-through-Friday schedule, which was hard to come by in the world of twenty-four-hour news. The switch seemed like a no-brainer, except for public perception.

"Demotion? Promotion?" That was the newspaper's gossip-column headline the day after it was announced I had stepped down from my weekend anchor job to take a position hosting a weekday morning lifestyle show. What? Leave prime time? I had achieved a coveted position only to give it up for a job on a show that was viewed as a lesser product. And people laughed at me.

"We don't see you much anymore," said an usher at church one Sunday morning after the closing prayer.

"I'm here every Sunday," I responded, knowing full well he was referring to my on-air repositioning. His comment hurt a little, especially since I had always thought of a church as a safe haven, and I didn't even know the guy!

"Didn't you *used* to be on TV?" asked a stranger at the mall.

"I still am," was the only response I could muster.

Oh, how my ego suffered one hit after another. Here I was supposed to be climbing the ladder, and I had intentionally stepped down a rung or two, an uncommon move in the competitive world of TV news. I found myself constantly having to explain myself. That was when I started to die.

I started to die to my ego, to the forces that tell you you're nothing without title and position.

I began to define myself not by what I did (report the news on TV) but by who I was (a mom). I will never forget what happened one morning when I was dropping off Jared at the childcare center. I had just said goodbye and was walking out the door. Another mom was heading in. As she saw me, she gasped, and I thought she was going to say, "You're that lady on TV!" like so many people had said to me before. Instead, she exclaimed, "You're Jared's mom!"

"Yes," I said. "I am."

Like so many other working moms, I had simply made a personal decision that I believed would help me achieve what was most important to me at the time: balance. It was a decision I made in part but not just because I was a single mom (and not because I was in some sort of "predicament" as someone actually stated to my face). I made that decision because I felt I was missing seeing my son grow up. The babysitter knew more about his likes and dislikes than I did. He was in day care during the day and with a babysitter on the weekends.

Mondays and Tuesdays were my days off, and Mondays became known as "Mommy and Jared Day." We went to the park, the children's museum, the movies, and, in the summer, to the beach. That was our day and my way of staying connected with my son. But for some reason, it just wasn't enough. I was still missing a big chunk of his life on the weekends, and I still wasn't going to church on Sundays. After a little more than a year of anchoring weekends, I'd had enough of missing my son.

While it's true I was no longer prime time, working midmornings gave me the balance I needed to make my life work, and what the scoffers, naysayers, and gossipers failed to realize was that the new position, though not as prestigious, still came with a raise.

Somebody somewhere was looking out for me.

God had smiled on me, again.

A few months into the morning position, I got to know a travel expert who was a regular on the show. He would mention how much he always enjoyed being interviewed by me and then one summer he met my son at the State Fair. Sometime after that, he stopped by my desk and dropped off a travel itinerary. I asked him what it was. He looked at me and said, "You just won the lottery. Don't dance with any strange men." I picked up the itinerary, and inside were two tickets for an all-expenses-paid Disney cruise to the Bahamas. Even though every now and then station talent, as they called us, were offered opportunities to go on promotional trips, and on rare occasions take family members, I couldn't believe that I was the one chosen for this trip—and that I'd be able to take my son!

First the raise, and now a trip. After working so hard trying to hold it all together, here was another gift from heaven. I knew this was going to be the trip of a lifetime, and it was.

We had the time of our lives. During our days at sea, Jared would swim in the deck pool while I read on a lounge chair nearby. We ate tons and tons of ice cream and pizza, and on the days when

71

we would dock at different ports of call and ferry to land for shore excursions, we would swim in crystal-blue ocean water and eat barbeque under grass umbrellas.

At the end of each day, we'd climb into small boats and ferry back to the ship. I'd make sure he'd get a nap, and then we'd get dressed for dinner: a collared shirt for him and a sundress for me. We'd walk up the ship's spiral staircase to one of several dining rooms, just me and my little boy.

I look back now, and I remember how the two of us attracted a bit of attention from the other families on the ship. It never dawned on me that being a single mom on a cruise with her son seemed odd. In my eyes, we were a family just like everybody else. I sat by the pool and watched my kid swim just like other parents did. When we were at different ports of call, I made sure to stuff his backpack with juice and water, sunscreen, and his favorite toy, the way any other parent of a young child would.

To me, being a single parent made me no less of a parent. I was determined that Jared and I were not going to become a statistic, the kind that often made it into my news scripts back at the station. The statistics filled with grim projections about my son's future; "facts" that implied brown little boys who grew up in single parent homes were less likely to graduate from high school and more likely to end up in prison or dead. Whenever I read these stats, it would just break my heart. I was almost defiant and certainly determined to prove those stats wrong. I wanted to give my son every chance at succeeding in life. I wanted him to discover and explore and be exposed to things that would make him dream and realize just how big and full of promises the world could be, and that's what this cruise was all about.

One night we got all dressed up for the captain's dinner. I had on a long, sparkly, black dress, and I dressed Jared in a pair of khaki pants, a white shirt, and a tie. I remember we took pictures under the spiral staircase with Mickey Mouse, then went up into the dining room for dinner. Afterward, we walked along the deck of the ship. The stars had just come out to play, and a full moon sat in a deep-purple evening sky, casting a wide swath of light onto the open sea. I could see the whitecaps and hear the *shhh, shhh-shh-ing* sounds as the massive ship cut through the deep ocean water. A cool mist was blowing, and we could smell the ocean air. My son had untucked his shirt from his pants and was playing shuffleboard on the deck of the ship as his tie and shirttails flapped in the night wind. The black silk scarf I had tied around my neck had also caught the ocean breeze. I looked at all of this on this moonlit night—me, my son, the ship, the ocean—and I asked God, how did we ever find ourselves here? A lonely single mom and her handsome little boy. Only God knows why we had been blessed with such a wonderful opportunity. I felt like we were in heaven.

73

A few years later, *Working Mother* magazine called.

I had subscribed to the magazine for years and joined their readers' panel. From time to time they would poll the moms on the panel about such topics as bedtime rituals, picky eaters, child care, or temper tantrums—all the things parents of young children face—and ask us how we dealt with these issues. I would write short little blurbs and e-mail them to the editors. Sometimes a sentence or two of mine would get published, which was a big thrill for me. The first time I got quoted was in an article on how parents spoil their children (something, admittedly, I may have been guilty of at times).

Not too long after that, the magazine announced an essay contest:

Dear Readers' Panel member,

Forget celebrities. Will you be the next "real mom" on the cover of Working Mother *magazine?*

Working Mother turns twenty-five next year, and in honor of our anniversary, we want to salute the kind of women who got us here. Working Mother magazine is all about real women, so who better to feature on the cover every month?

We're going to fly nine lucky readers to New York City next year for exclusive photo shoots—and one of them could be you. If you're selected, you'll be shot by a top New York photographer. We'll style your hair, do your makeup, even dress you up—all you have to do is HAVE FUN!

We'll also feature you and your children inside the magazine, on our "Why Do You Work?" page. A photographer will come to your town to take pictures of you and your kids in a setting that illustrates what you do for a living.

Thank you!
The Editors at Working Mother

Wow, I thought, *now wouldn't that be fun?* I knew exactly why I worked. I worked to live instead of living to work. The changes I had made in my schedule had provided enough balance for me to do a little bit of a lot of the things I loved. I loved working in television, and I was on it. Granted, it wasn't prime time, but I still had a job in the field I loved. I loved parenting, and I was doing it, in the morning, after school, at dinner and bedtime each night. I spent time in my garden. I could go to church on Sunday. Spend time with my friends. After making so many decisions to get here, my life was finally working. And so that 150-word essay was a breeze.

Dear Working Mother *magazine,*

Work allows me to be who I am: curious, creative, and a better parent.

As host of a daily lifestyle television show, my job is a constant education. I've learned how to cook and garden!

My schedule also allows me valuable time to be with my son. Balance.

I am so grateful to be able to make a living. As a single parent, I know what the statistics say. How difficult it is to go it alone… the plague poverty can play on children raised in single-parent homes. I thank God every day for a job that not only pays the mortgage, but also allows me to tuck a little away for my son's future.

I know I am fortunate to have overcome a setback, work in a field I love, and provide for my son. I work because it allows me to be who I am.

The following Sunday at church, I told my pastor I was going to enter the contest and that I had written about how having balance in my life helped me to be a happy parent. I remember him saying very emphatically, "You are going to win!" It was as if God himself had said it.

"You are going to win!"

With that prophetic blessing, I found a black-and-white head shot of myself (the one that prompted some people to say my pixie haircut made me look like Halle Berry), and I mailed the essay and photo to *Working Mother* magazine and then completely forgot about it.

Two months later, it was early October. The sun was lower in the sky, and the days were shorter and cooler. I remember that day so vividly. My son and I had just gotten home from school and work, and we would have the next few days off for conferences and fall break.

We came into the house, and I sent Jared off to do homework while I went into the kitchen to see what could be made into dinner. *Spaghetti? Pizza? Chicken? What's in the freezer?* Decided spaghetti would do, all the ingredients were there. As I was getting the noodles out of the cabinet I checked my phone messages. One call. Area code 212.

212? That's odd. How could a telemarketer get through? I thought. I had blocks on the phone. I didn't put it together until I listened to the message. 212 is a New York area code.

"Hello, Roxane, this is *Working Mother* magazine. We're calling about a letter you sent. Could you give us a call at your earliest convenience?"

Oh. My. God. Could this be? No. Yes? Maybe?

Since the call came at the end of the businesses day, I would have to wait until the following morning to return it.

That night, trying to get to sleep was torture. All sorts of thoughts played through my mind.

No, it can't be.

Don't get your hopes up.

Maybe they're calling to say thank you, but no thank you.

What? What do they want? Could it be?

No.

Yes.

77

Maybe.

Just believe, Roxane.

Weary and tired and finally ready for sleep, I thought, *Just let go, and believe.*

Three weeks later I was in New York City.

I had gotten a facial, gotten my hair done, and whitened my teeth. I remember my curls bouncing up and down as I walked through Chicago's O'Hare International Airport on my way to my connecting flight to New York.

During my layover, I sucked it all in.

"Your attention, please. In the interest of aviation safety, all bags are subject to search." The recorded voice was a woman with an English accent.

"Parents, for safety reasons, please take responsibility for your children." The British woman again. Her o's more rounded than flat. I often wondered why the "voice" of Chicago O'Hare was British. Wasn't this the Midwest?

Across the wide terminal came the soft hiss of the cappuccino machine, the rattle of coffee beans hitting the metal grinder; the quiet order of the adjacent bookstore, colorful and symmetrical as soft-spoken clerks quietly restocked best sellers, pulling literary hopefuls and treasures from green plastic bins and placing them onto their designated shelves. New Releases. Famous Authors.

All the while, the innocuous yet constant low rumble of the people movers were heard only if you listened, along with low but audible cell phone chatter: the who and why of what occurred while you were away or when you got there.

"Okay, great. I'll call you when I'm back in the office on Monday."

"Wheelchair assistance needed at gate A-1." The woman with the British accent was gone. In her place: a live female voice, strained but controlled with a hint of a southern drawl. "Wheelchair assistance needed at gate A-1, please."

Finally the call came to board my flight. Standing in the jetway, I could feel the chill of the rainy late October afternoon. I watched out the window as the gray overcast, which had lingered all day and produced a steady cold drizzle, engulfed one plane after another; then the slow angular ascents, noses upward, disappearing into the gray mist moments after takeoff. The loud steely roar of aircraft engines filled the sky. Onboard and buckled in, I slept for most of the three-hour flight out east.

When I arrived at the LaGuardia Airport, a Hispanic gentlemen in a dark gray suit, black tie, and white shirt was waiting in baggage claim among all the other chauffeurs. The sign that he carried said "Battle." That was my name, and he was there for me.

He grabbed my one bag from the baggage claim, and moments later I was in the backseat of a shiny black Lincoln Town Car. Unreal. Not even in the back of that town car, in the dark New York streets, did I feel fear. Fatigue, yes—I had been traveling most of the day—but fear, no. Not yet.

The magazine had put me up at the Marcel, a nice boutique hotel in Manhattan's Gramercy neighborhood. It had high ceilings with heavy metal doors painted in muted neutral tones. After I checked in and was finally alone in my room, then I was afraid.

The room is so small. The bed is so big. Will the lock on the metal door hold? I was there all alone, in an area of New York I'd never been. Yes, I had traveled to New York City numerous times in my life, but always to reconnect with familiar faces. Here I was now, in a strange room, preparing to meet strange faces. They had flown me here, sight unseen, except for a black-and-white photograph.

What if they don't like me?

What if they're not nice?

Even worse, what if they're mean?

Is this really for real?

I, however, was at the point of no return. All I could do now was crawl underneath the white cotton duvet of the queen-size hotel bed and pray for sleep.

"Ms. Battle, your car is ready."

"Thank you," I replied the next morning to the voice calling from the hotel's front desk. My tone tried to conceal the fact that this was the first time in my life anyone had ever said that to me.

80   Your car is ready. It was 9:05 a.m.

The magazine editors had said the car would pick me up at 9:10. *Strange time*, I thought. *Why not 9:15?* It didn't matter. I was ready.

After a fitful night of what would have to pass for sleep, I was showered and dressed, ready for my big day.

I wore a pair of Gap boot-cut blue jeans and a three-quarter-length suede fringed jacket over a black-and-red beaded top. *This is as good an outfit as any to make a first impression*, I thought. *Be yourself. Relaxed and informal. With just a hint of personal style.*

The hotel lobby was now a hub, unlike the night before when I had checked in after midnight. Now businessmen in suit jackets and ties were coming and going, reading the paper and sipping coffee from white paper cups. Several black town cars sat parked in front, waiting to dispatch and deliver.

Here I was, a visitor from the Midwest, a part of it all. Back home I had been told I was too ethnic, too exotic. Here, amid the various dialects and ethnicities, I fit right in. New York was both fascinating and familiar. My surroundings, coupled with the anticipation of my photo shoot, were as exhilarating as they were anxiety-provoking.

Seven past nine, three minutes early, I thought as I settled into the back of the town car, proud of myself that on this day, my habitual ten-minute tardiness had reversed itself. Yellow taxis, black town cars, and white delivery trucks all made their way through noisy, narrow, and crowded New York streets. Thin thoroughfares carved out between towering concrete.

The car deposited me in front of a stone-colored building. "Eagle's Nest, ma'am," said the driver in a thick Middle-Eastern accent. I signed the voucher, climbed out of the car, and there I was again, alone on a New York City street. Once again: fear.

Is this the right address?

Where's the building entrance?

Can people tell I'm not from here?

I looked at the notes I had written down: *Eagle's Nest photography studio, 259 West 30th Street.* This was it.

I pushed number thirteen once inside the elevator, and just as the door was about to close, three more people got in, a woman and two men, all in their early thirties. The woman, with a thick blonde ponytail and wearing a yellow-hooded rain jacket, was carrying a white handbag with patch pockets that I had seen in a fall fashion magazine. I wanted to compliment her on the bag as we rode up to the thirteenth floor, but she was having so much fun being friendly to the two gentlemen she was with that I didn't dare interrupt.

"She's going to thirteen," she said, referring to me. "We're going to *four*."

A laugh followed, and then some witty comment about the merits, or the lack thereof, of the fourth floor. Happy morning chatter between friendly strangers. Or were they coworkers? Were they graphic designers? Photographers? *What will* they *be doing all day?* I wondered. The friendly, easy tone of their conversation suggested to me they might be some creative types: thinkers, creators, dreamers.

Like me.

Ding. The fourth floor, and they were gone.

I checked my hair one more time in the mirrored reflection of the elevator walls I rode up alone to thirteen. The photography studio seemed to take up an entire floor. There was a small reception area that opened into an expansive loft with worn hardwood floors, high ceilings, white-washed walls, and natural light. As soon as I walked in and said my name, the reaction from a nice young woman in jeans and a sweater made it clear they were expecting me.

"Roxane! Oh yes, right this way," she said as I followed her to a dressing room tucked in the back of the studio, where a male makeup artist was waiting.

"Do you know any vegan men?" he asked just moments after I settled into his makeup chair. I was less startled than flattered. He had just started working on my face, and he actually felt comfortable asking me if I knew any eligible men. Maybe he was just trying to make me feel comfortable so I'd be relaxed for the shoot. I didn't know any vegan men, and I told him so.

"Oh well." He sighed melodramatically as he flicked black powder off an eyebrow brush. "Never give up," he said, more to himself than me. His never was more of a nevuh. He was Brooklyn born and raised, and looking for the partner he knew was out there. *I'm just not going there today,* I thought. Relationships can be complicated enough, why add dietary restrictions?

I would later learn he asked the vegan question with the same regularity that he cleaned his brushes. It was habit. Each new face that sat in his chair got the same question.

His makeup kit was a silver-colored metal case. Inside, the lid was lined with oblong black leather pouches. Each pouch held long and thin brushes, identical except for their varying sizes. The case rested on the windowsill beneath the window he used to make me up in natural light, and inside the bottom were neatly arranged acrylic square containers, each holding his palette of colors. One for lips, one for blushes. He was so neat and organized, I thought, and meticulous. He took over an hour to do my face. He painted in my eyebrow hairs one at a time with a brush so thin and delicate I barely felt it on my skin. He was wearing a black cotton short-sleeve shirt and black slacks that couldn't hide the fact that he was very thin. Vegan. No meat, no dairy. *Perhaps a little protein wouldn't be all that bad*, I thought.

On a rack behind the makeup chair was an array of cashmere and wool sweaters, in soft creams and pastels.

The wardrobe stylist ditched the beaded top I was wearing but loved my jeans. They put me in an oatmeal-color sweater for the first of what would be nearly a dozen wardrobe changes.

"We're going to snap another Polaroid before we go to film," said the photographer, a petite Indian woman dressed in an army-green cable-knit sweater and matching pants.

"We're losing the light…." More clicks of the camera shutter.

"Gorge!" That was her favorite word, short for *gorgeous*.

"Gorge!" I heard that with more and more frequency as the afternoon rolled on.

They fed me bagels and cream cheese for breakfast and chicken lo mein and spring rolls for lunch. At one point during the photo shoot, late in the afternoon, they asked me if I wanted anything else to eat or drink.

I remember feeling like I might be coming down with a cold, so I asked for a cup of hot green tea. The magazine editor herself, who had been supervising the shoot, made a cup of tea in the kitchen area in a far corner of the spacious studio, and then, being careful not to spill it, very slowly carried it across the studio floor to where I was sitting in front of the camera and studio lights. When she handed me the cup and saucer, I burst into tears. I sobbed and sobbed, ruining the makeup they had applied, and dripping black-mascara-tinted tears onto the outfit I was wearing—just sobbing and sobbing. I was overcome by all these strange people who were being so incredibly nice to me. I was so overwhelmed that *Working Mother* had flown me, a single mom from Minneapolis, to New York to put me on the cover of a national magazine. I just sobbed and sobbed.

Through gasps I thanked them and said I couldn't believe how nice this all was and how wonderful this was, and what an amazing experience this was, sob, sob, and sob. They all gathered around me, the photographer, the makeup artist, the editor, and patted my back and shoulders. They told me that all the other moms who had won the contest and come to New York for their photo sessions had done the exact same thing—sobbed.

85

Right then and there, every decision I had made up to that point had been worth it. I had made decisions in an effort to bring balance into my life, but those decisions would also mean I would never be prime time, and my face would never be on the side of a city bus or local billboard. But by some amazing turn of events, I did end up on the cover a national magazine.

A month later, Ebony *magazine flew into town. They took several poses of me and Jared, many very similar to what* Working Mother *had shot, including a pose where my son was wearing a headset and pointing to the camera's teleprompter, which read, "And now back to you, Mom." We would be part of a six-page spread on successful career moms.*

5

BLACK EYED PEAS AND BASKETBALL

*He who begets a wise child will delight in him. Let your father
and your mother be glad, and let her who bore you rejoice.*
—Proverbs 23:24–25

"We did it! We did it. We're on a di-et," we sang as we turned
the corner into the Eagan High School parking lot.

Jared cracked up every time we imitated the funny freckled fish
Dory from the Disney animated movie *Finding Nemo*.

"We did it! We did it!"

Fifteen minutes early and we didn't get lost this time, although
I did stop once at the Citgo to show the gas station attendant my
map and ask her if I was going the right way. Turned out I was less
than a mile from the school.

It was his first basketball tournament. Fifth-grade traveling B
team, Hopkins Royals. Tip off, 8:00 p.m. Coach Tim said to be
there by 7:30. We pulled into the parking lot at 7:15.

"We did it, Jared!" I said. "And Mama's even early!"

"Good job, Mom," he said. Having watched me over the years struggle with map reading and punctuality, Jared was used to being late and benefiting from yet another teachable moment: *See, Son, even adults have things they need to work on.*

"C'mon, Mom; let's go, Mom!"

"Okay, buddy."

Out of the car, into the dark, cool, early November night, we made our way toward the building, immediately immersed in a tiny city of ball players funneling into the white-lighted entrance of the mammoth school, all of them wearing various colors of sweatshirts and hoodies emblazoned with district logos, with matching sweatpants and ball bags.

"Craft Show Saturday and Sunday 9 a.m. to 4 p.m." A sign and an arrow explained why the parking lot was so full. There by the entrance were double-parked trucks and trailers with their back doors open, burgeoning with pull carts and plastic bins.

We followed the crowd inside. The rustic orange cinder-block walls seemed much higher than I remembered from my days in school, but then again, that was a long time ago. The pull carts were turning to the left down a hallway, past the restrooms and water fountains, to set up for the next day's craft show in the cafeteria. It was Friday night, and we headed to the right, toward the smell of mini-donuts and the gym.

"Two dollars, please." *That's right*, I thought. This was traveling ball, no more freebies like parks and rec. I handed over the two bills for my admission.

"Thank you, have a good game," and we were in. Jared was wide-eyed and so was I. Inside the gym, blue dividers split the hardwood into three courts. Three games. Fourth quarter. Parents and siblings crammed together in folding chairs along one side; on the other side, sweaty, pink-cheeked preteens filled out the team bench.

"Travel! Blue ball!" followed the shrill of the gray-haired ref's whistle.

On each side of the blue divider: noise, balls, buzzers' shrills, applause, and the sound of sneaker-clad size fives and sixes pounding up and down the court. Tank tops and numbered nylon. This was traveling basketball.

88

I looked at Jared, who had found a spot on the edge of the court to soak it all in. Dressed in his trademark knit beanie and royal-blue sweatshirt and sweatpants, he had grabbed his right foot and was doing hamstring stretches, just like he had seen the pros do on TV. He wanted to be so much like them, in every way.

We would play out this scene over and over again throughout the winter and into the early spring. One traveling basketball tournament after another, Friday nights, Saturday mornings, and Sunday afternoons, until we would finally make our way to the granddaddy of them all, the tournament in Rochester, Minnesota, home of the world-renowned Mayo Clinic and travel-league basketball. Each year, during the first weekend in March, that small town of gray skyscrapers and aging hotels hosted one of the largest basketball tournaments in the state.

In the spring of his sixth-grade year, we made the two-hour drive from the Twin Cities heading east on Highway 55, a straight shot, passing through dormant snow-covered cornfields and small Midwestern towns: Zumbrota, Wanamingo, Mazeppa. Jared worked the CD player with his favorite discs, Beyoncé and the Black Eyed Peas. I had actually bought him the Black Eyed Peas CD after seeing a network profile piece on the group's success story. I thought the lyrics in "Where Is the Love?" had a good message. But I should have listened to the rest of the CD. Since when did music include cuss words! Whatever happened to the songs I used to listen to? I could not believe the stuff that was on the radio, especially the rap songs, which Jared loved. I tried to steer him toward more wholesome music, checking out gospel rap CDs at the church bookstore. Still, edited versions of his secular favorites were our compromise.

89

We pulled into Rochester at dusk, just as the streetlights began to twinkle, along with the rest of the Hopkins 5B team caravan. The lobby of the Kahler Inn and Suites was overrun with royal-blue sweatpants and hoodies, caps and sweatshirts, loyal family members and fans of the Hopkins boys' traveling basketball league, which marked the beginning of the journey toward esteemed varsity ball. Hopkins's program was renowned throughout the state. Ranked fourteenth in the country, it had produced a number of Division I ball players, some of whom had gone on to play for the University of Minnesota Gophers, and from there, to rookie opportunities in the NBA. Kris Humphries, of Kim Kardashian fame, was one of them.

The Hopkins league was an elite program, one of prestige, and the Rochester tournament was a rite of passage. The entire program was here, ninety-eight ball players, grades five through eight, along with their coaches and parents, who, in anticipation of the long weekend, had discreetly packed poker chips and coolers of beer.

Jared's experience with traveling basketball had, at this point, stretched to five months and far too few wins. Each weekend we'd load up the car with gas and a duffel bag and travel long distances on day trips to Elk River, Shakopee, Eagan, Apple Valley, Edina, or Eden Prairie for what seemed to be one endless drubbing. Each time, the boys were outmatched and outrun, and now here we were on our first overnight trip to Rochester, the one tournament Jared had looked forward to all season long. A mini-March Madness. Rematches with teams from all over the region. A rewrite of the season's play-by-play.

Over the course of the season, Jared's team, Hopkins 5B, had evolved from strangers to a special group of friends.

There was curly-haired Eli, who, when he was on, astonished his teammates with the ease and consistency with which he nailed three-pointers. He would become our MVP. His father—with his second wife and their two young daughters—and his mother would alternate coming to games. Sometimes they'd all show up at the same game at the same time, with mom sitting on one side of the center-court line, ex-hubby and family number two sitting on the other. It somewhat reminded me of my own situation, although my ex-husband and I were now cordial enough to sit next to each other at games every now and then. But most of the time I sat center court, which gave me an unrestricted view of the bench and both baskets. I liked that. Jared's father, always with some sort of electronic device in tow, either a video or Canon still camera, preferred to position himself near one of the baskets.

Luke, a fourth grader, had earned a fifth-grade spot through talented, consistent play and nearly flawless layups. Round-faced and hazel-eyed, he had the looks and God-given talent of a natural-born star. Noah was so small and dark-haired, the boys nicknamed him "Elf." "Tabasco" was another one of his monikers because he played with such flushed-faced passion and intensity.

Sam, who could be counted on to find a spot on the low post and bank it in, had missed the last two tournaments because of an extremely rare case of croup. His four-year-old sister, with dark eyes and a pixie haircut, looked just like him. Little Natalie would make the rounds of the moms and dads during the game, always wearing the cutest little outfits. Leopard- and zebra-print appeared to be her (or her mother's) favorite.

Patrick's dad was the team parent, calling or e-mailing us throughout the week to remind us of practice times and locations, picture day, and tournament dates. Both father and son were extremely kind, consistent, and dependable. Patrick's free throws landed so often, the boys called him "And One." Patrick's mother rarely came to the games, and I often wondered if that might be the reason for the hints of sadness in his father's eyes.

And finally Carnell, aka Corndog, was the only black kid on the team who started. He lived in the apartment complex across from the district offices and had a game born of the streets. With the build of a sixth grader, he was much larger and stronger than the other boys. The three hundred dollars it cost to join the league had been a great sacrifice for his parents, who never missed a game. We all watched 'Nell develop from a showy ball hog into a team player who could be counted on in the clutch.

There was no question these boys had game. What they didn't have was a plan. They were individual kids who had to be transformed into a team by Coach Curry.

Coming out of the stands to coach from the bench, Coach Curry began his transformation midseason, at a time when parents were frustrated by spending their weekends suffering through games that were noncompetitive at best, brutal and disheartening at worst. Playing three to four games a weekend, we were lucky to win one, but we could never hope to truly contend, much less earn coveted hardware: medals and trophies. Having had enough of empty-handedness, a few parents, including myself and Noah's dad, wrote polite but stern letters to the league board. The student-coaches, we wrote, while nice young men (two sixteen-year-olds who'd been cut from the varsity team), were too inexperienced, and at times too distracted (translation: *girls*), to teach our boys the fundamentals of the game.

Coach Curry had coached eighth-grade basketball for twelve years, winning championships and accolades. He had grown up in the district, the high school's first-ever black homecoming king. His picture, all these years later, was still posted in a hall display case at his high school alma mater. One had to look closely, however, since the Afro he'd worn was now a tightly cropped fade. But the toothy grin remained unchanged. He was a natural-born coach who couldn't talk without moving his hands and body. Eloquent and impassioned, he had envisioned a career in college ball but was diverted by a lack of height and a love of teaching. Coaching basketball allowed him to manifest his dream, keeping it alive vicariously. All the while he also dreamed of the day when his own son would be old enough to play traveling ball. That day had come.

And so the turnaround began. Coach Curry believed one didn't set out to win championships; one developed players first, and the championships would follow. Focus on improving individuals, and the team would take care of the rest. He was right. Over the next few weeks, we watched as the boys ran harder and played longer than they ever had. Jared came home exhausted each night after practice, crawling into bed after a late dinner and hot shower. In time, the team's playing style, thanks to repetitive drills and the cutting of the uncommitted, began to evolve from scattered happenstance, where individuals vied to be stars, to one of strategy, ball-sharing, and well-executed plays. Teamwork.

Jared had begun the season starting at point guard, hitting the first three-pointer of the season. But while struggling to grow into his long skinny limbs and overcome nervous jitters, he had been surpassed by teammates who were not necessarily quicker but were more sure-footed. His hands just couldn't seem to hang on to the ball. His body moved more quickly than his mind, which made for fast play that often resulted in missed layups and passes that became turnovers. I would pray Jared's turnovers wouldn't result in an opposing basket, but often they did. However, soon after Coach Curry took over, Jared began to answer back, stealing the ball on the next possession and either passing it for an assist or forging down the lane for a layup.

Coach now started Carnell at point guard, Luke small forward, and Eli at center. Noah and Patrick filled out the starting five. Jared came off the bench as the sixth man, part of the team's second unit. He had found his role—calling the plays while Carnell rested and assisting in more than his share of buckets. Though assigned to a lesser role, he began to make major contributions on the court. He had developed into a quick thinker who had learned how and when to pass the ball.

94

The boys were excited and hungry for a win. They had worked very hard every Monday, Tuesday, and Thursday night down in the junior high gym. And on this day, here on the flat windy plains of Rochester, Minnesota, that work bore fruit.

Eastview was our first opponent, a tight little basketball team that had made mincemeat out of us twice during the season and was favored to take it all. Their point guard, number thirty-four, was small but a demon on the fast break. And the rest of their boys had bulk. Eastview's half-court passes had beaten our boys to the bucket every time.

But this time Coach Curry's wind sprints, that series of much-hated killers—down and backs—paid off. As Eastview became winded, Hopkins kept pace, taking the lead early, then falling behind and catching up. At one point they let the lead slip by as much as sixteen points with four minutes left in the game, and we thought it was all over. But amazingly, in a show of determination that would become the highlight of the season, the boys rallied back.

Their play was passionate, their passes quick, their timing and instinct dead-on. No-look passes and miraculous three-point shots made for the most exciting play we had witnessed all season. Jared would drive the ball down the lane to within striking distance, find an open man, and pass it off, forming an arc above the three-point line, Jared to Luke, Luke to Noah, Noah to Patrick, back to Noah, up against the backboard, rimmed in for two. They were aggressive under the basket, our boys grabbing rebounds time and time again, Luke and Noah turning missed shots into possessions and points, Eli hitting his threes, and Carnell beating everybody to the basket for one layup after another.

He'd nail it, and each time parents would leap from the bleachers with cheers and applause.

"Way to go, Hopkins! Way to go!"

Across the court, the Eastview coaches had been on autopilot throughout the season, as if an Eastview win were inevitable, especially when tipping off against a scrawny team of non-contenders like ours. They seemed so confident in their team's ability, the coach and his assistant would often chill and laugh it up with friendly sideline chats. But today their smiles were replaced with furrowed brows of concern.

Time-out.

Our boys had brought the game to within two points, with a minute to go in the fourth quarter. I had started to pray. Eli's mom and I held hands. My eyes filled with tears as I looked back on the season.

How my son had walked off the court, game after game, his tired, sweaty face flushed, a loser again and again.

"The wins are coming, Son, the wins are coming," I would say. It was all I could do to give him hope. "As long as you know you gave it all you had," I would say on the ride home. "As long you know you left everything out there on the floor, you have nothing to hang your head about." But it was little consolation for a team that just couldn't seem to win. And now here we were, on the brink of not only a win, but an upset—tired, sweaty, and flush-faced.

"Hang in there, buddy; you can do it, J!" I yelled from the sideline.

"Let's go, Hopkins!"

Oh Lord, let 'em win this time. Let them win. They had worked so hard. A loss now would leave them absolutely shattered. The buzzer signaled the end of the fourth quarter. Luke had laid it in. Game tied 50–50.

My heart was thundering.

"Come on, you guys, this is ours!" Jared told his teammates during the huddle as the scoring table reset the clock to two minutes.

"This is ours; let's take it!"

He wanted to win. Badly.

"One, two, three, Hopkins!"

"Get home, Hopkins!" yelled Coach Curry. "Get home!"

Luke, then Carnell, both landed shots. Solid defense kept Eastview to just one bucket, and those two minutes quickly expired. It was over in overtime. Hopkins beat Eastview 54–52, knocking them out of championship contention, and giving our boys their first real taste of what it's like to take on and conquer a formidable opponent. An unlikely win for a team who would be underdogs no more.

In the end we took fourth at Rochester, but this time it was not our losses but wins that we would remember. After our final game Sunday afternoon, back at the hotel, I learned our boys had become the talk of the tournament. A tiny team of scrubs that had been politely tolerated and privately ridiculed all season had won, twice. There were no comers on this team, so they had said, no perceived contenders, only the least talented, the smallest, and weakest here to fill out a bracket, but never to be taken seriously. Yet they had won two tough games, back to back.

By contrast, the highly favored 5A team hadn't won a game all weekend. Immediately relegated to the consolation round, slugging it out through four games, sixteen quarters, all they walked away with was a bad memory. On top of that, no other Hopkins team playing in the Rochester tournament that year had beaten Eastview. But we had. Down by ten or more twice, we had come back to win both times. Out of sixteen teams, we had made it to the final four.

97

"I am so proud of you boys," said Coach. "It's one thing to be down, it's another to come back, keep coming back, the way you guys did. Sure, you could have gone out there and shot a bunch of three-pointers, but this was a game of character. You boys showed maturity and focus. I tell ya, I'm really proud of you boys."

Later that evening I made a run to Culver's for dinner, and in our hotel room, making short work of buffalo chicken tenders and a chocolate-mint shake, my boy weighed in.

"So, Jared, how do you think you did?" I asked.

"Today?" he said, taking a bite of his chicken finger.

"Today…and overall."

98

"Well…," his eyes rolled upward thoughtfully as he took another bite of chicken. "At the beginning of the season, we sucked."

"True."

"I thought you said we were good at the beginning of the season, Mom!"

"You were!" I backpedaled. "You had potential to be good. I could see it. You just needed to be uh…coached…uh…developed. The potential was there all the time. Kinda like the chicken and the egg. First the chicken lays the egg, and uh, you know, it's just an egg until, uh, you know, the egg has the potential to be a chicken."

I was fumbling all over myself. "You know what I mean, Son. So anyway, how do you think you did?"

"Can I tell you something, Mom?"

"Yeah, buddy."

"We just hatched."

The true triumph of the season was not the championship trophy but the fact that this fifth grader had come through all of the flush-faced losses and disappointments and recognized his growth and development. He had produced his own pocket of joy, seeing progress for himself, through his own eyes, and was proud. Even though the ultimate prize had eluded him, he and the Hopkins 5B team had gained something much more—confidence—and there, on the windy plains of Rochester, that was enough.

"We just hatched, Mom. We just hatched."

99

The next weekend, we traveled to Hastings to play in our last tournament of the season. State. We won two games, advancing and winning a third to take Big Lake 23–20 for the state championship.

6

SPALDING NEVERFLAT
An Essay by My Son, Jared

Think of this chapter as a time-out, or better yet, half time. It wasn't written by me, but instead by Jared. It belongs here, in a book about our family, because it provides insight that only he could give about basketball and, more importantly, his relationship with his father.

The summer after sixth grade was hotter than any other one I had experienced in the past. Rain wouldn't come for weeks at a time, and the temperature would stay in the nineties and hundreds more often than not. My friends and I couldn't wait to use the residents' pool that was a couple hundred yards away from my mom's house, like we had in previous summers.

We would all be attending junior high in the fall, so it was a time of transition to new responsibilities. While other soon-to-be seventh graders were reminiscing about the good times they had had in elementary school and slathering on sunscreen, I could focus only on my jump shot and my ball handling. Basketball was a way of life for me at that age, and since my last season was sort of a flop, I had to do everything in my power to unlock the potential that my dad had always told me I had.

I managed to make the A team after tryouts, but the rest of the season didn't seem to go my way. All of the playing time I didn't get over the season and mistakes I made during games seemed to be on repeat in my head when I would practice. It probably didn't help that my dad recorded all the games so we could rewind and view each and every play until I saw exactly what I did wrong.

"You know, you could be a better player than I ever was, Jared. It all depends on how hard you're willing to work," my dad stated confidently. He played basketball at Kansas State University in his college days, which made him the most credible source of basketball knowledge I knew.

"But I do work hard, Dad. I come to the gym with you every morning!" I replied.

"I don't think you know what hard work is yet, Son."

I stayed silent as I imagined myself playing and practicing more basketball than I already did on a daily basis, then shivered at the thought of not playing as much PlayStation as usual. Thinking he was all talk, I inquired, "So how much did you practice?"

"Three, maybe four times a day. Practicing once and then playing NBA video games all day isn't how you do it."

He shut me up again. I never liked how much he hated to watch me play video games for more than an hour, but I couldn't help thinking there was some truth to his snappy remark.

We had just left Lifetime Fitness and were on our way to Olive Garden, my dad's favorite place to eat at the time. As we waited in the sunny parking lot for our carryout order, I let my eyes wander around my surroundings and fixated on the Sports Authority right across the lot from where we were. Suddenly, I remembered a commercial I had seen about a new basketball and its innovative technology. "The Spalding NeverFlat Basketball: Newly invented technology inside the ball prevents air from ever escaping. Even when it's cold! Now available at Sports Authority." The commercial was in my head as if someone had put it there.

"Hey, Dad?" I said in an innocent voice, in an effort to disguise the fact that I was about to ask for something.

"Yeah?"

"I don't have any good basketballs to use when I practice at home."

"Don't you have a zillion in the garage that you never use?" he asked, knowing my usual routine when asking for something new.

"Yeah, but all those ones aren't real good ones. I need a ball that you could use during a game if you had to."

102

"OK. I guess if you're going to start taking this seriously.... Let's see if they have it over there," he said as he pointed to Sports Authority.

I didn't rip open the light-blue, lightning-bolt-covered packaging until I got home, just to make the moment of unwrapping as epic as possible. After tearing away the cardboard I spun the ball in my hands a few times, focusing on the feel of the fresh dots landscaping each panel of the new ball. The grip on the ball was so strong and sticky that I could feel the friction heating up my fingertips as I watched the Spalding logo spin about.

"I love this ball," I said, thinking out loud.

"You should probably write your name on it, so you don't lose it at the gym," Dad suggested.

"Smart idea," I replied while rifling through his desk drawer. A traditional black Sharpie wouldn't do the job this time, as this wasn't just any old basketball. This was the ball I was finally going to become good with, the ball that would help me be a presence on my next team and prove everyone wrong. This ball was the beginning of hard work.

A giant ultrathick green Sharpie that had just been taken out of the box was the only one that seemed to fit the occasion. I painstakingly printed my first and last names along with my cell phone number just under the panel that had the Spalding logo.

"Neat enough?" Dad chuckled at the sight of my face so close to the ball all I could smell was Sharpie. It looked like I was trying to paint the Sistine Chapel with a marker.

103

"I don't wanna make any mistakes, Dad. This ball is important."

"I suppose. But it's what you do with it that's important." He clearly didn't think the ball was as awesome as I did.

The ball came with me everywhere. If I wasn't dribbling it, it was either in my lap when I was sitting down or under one of my arms as I walked. In the mornings, Dad and I would get to the gym and shoot baskets before the adults came in for their pickup games and the courts filled with sweaty competition. We would try to get at least one hundred jump shots up before it got crowded. When the games finally started, I would sit on a bench and dribble the ball underneath my legs to a very precise rhythm until something else I could do with the ball interested me.

I remember being told to get off the court by a bald yet very hairy gentleman and being banished to that cold metal bench just to wait for the ten-minute break between games when the hoops would be free again. Every now and then, kids would show up with their dads, but my dad made it my obligation to challenge one of them to a game of one-on-one. Losing such a personal battle was one of my biggest fears at that time, other than confrontation.

One day my dad pointed out a taller, more built middle schooler with bright-blond hair and a jump shot that was much better than mine. I had been watching him for a couple of minutes and wasn't excited to challenge him at all.

"But Dad, what if I lose?" I whined, my morale destroyed after he insisted I challenge the older competitor.

"I hope you don't expect to get better by winning all the time," he said as he shoved my ball into my stomach, making it clear that his request wasn't an option.

Losing games like that one became my biggest source of improvement that summer. As the school year approached, my dribbling became much more precise, and I was finally strong enough to shoot a three-pointer. After days at the gym, I would throw on one of several Nike headbands that I had and dribble up and down the street in the hot sun. My back had a red tint to it because of all the sunscreen I didn't put on, and my hands were covered in dirty calluses from every bounce of the NeverFlat. I began to challenge any and every kid that came through the door at Lifetime Fitness, and I was confident that I was going to win, as long as we played with my ball. My skill increase was so noticeable that sometimes I'd be allowed to play with my dad and other adults at the gym. Even though they all were three times my size, they could never get the ball from me. As I'd weave in and out of giant defenders who seemed to be standing still, and trick grown men with a fake that my dad had taught me, I knew that I had spent my time with the ball wisely.

When the time for tryouts came that fall, Dad made sure we were there an hour early. I didn't question it, until he took me to the outdoor hoops of the elementary school where the tryout would be. The outdoor courts had massive cracks in the pavement that made the ground uneven, and the net was made of chains. Every time I made a shot, the chains would jingle together for a few seconds like some sort of applause for all my effort that summer. Even with the wind blowing strong, I couldn't miss a shot that morning.

105

"If you keep shooting like this, you should have no problem at tryouts," Dad said encouragingly. There was more seriousness in his voice than anything.

"I don't think I've ever shot like this," I said as I felt the NeverFlat leave my hands and swoosh through the basket.

"You're more than ready for tryouts this year."

My seventh-grade tryout was a dream because of the work my dad and I had put in. Every move came off flawlessly in front of the coaches who would ultimately decide the path of my next season. Over those three days of tryouts, I simply could not have played better.

Jared made the A team that fall and played travel-league basketball until high school, where he played JV ball before switching to track and field. His senior year of high school, he went on to become captain of the track team and state champion. He wrote this essay for an English comp class his freshman year in college.

And now back to our regularly scheduled programming.

7

TIDAL WAVE

Be anxious for nothing but in everything by prayer and supplication, with thanksgiving, let your requests be made known to God; and the peace of God, which surpasses all understanding, will guard your hearts and minds through Jesus Christ.
—Philippians 4:6–7

By 2006, I had worked nearly twenty years in broadcast television news, I had seen it all, and now the station was asking me to do it again, with less, for less. The television news industry was in huge transition. The Internet had struck and was wreaking havoc. Viewing habits, established at the very beginning of television, were turned upside down. The television station I was working for, like many stations across the country, faced shrinking audiences and diminishing advertising revenue. We didn't know it at the time, but it was the end of an era. Television news would never again be the same.

The combination of budget cuts and clamoring egos had turned the newsroom into a toxic, negative-energy-driven, survival-of-the-fittest wasteland, a vortex of fear and frustration-fueled competitiveness, with every man and woman for themselves. What we had done before wasn't working anymore, and we were genuinely perplexed at the looming uncertainty the online world had brought. Station managers went into defense mode, trying to shore up shrinking budgets by generating more revenue, and I was one of their targets.

At the time, I was pulling double duty, working as both a host for the morning lifestyle show and as a news reporter. I'd host the show in the morning, then report in the afternoon. I had been at the television station for nearly thirteen years. I was making a six-figure income; I had great health insurance, a 401k, and money in the bank. That's when station management, made the decision to start charging guests to be on the show I cohosted. Show guests became "clients," and our community-friendly lifestyle show became an infomercial, or as the newly coined phrase at the time called it, "info-tainment."

My bosses gave me the choice of staying with the show for a much lower salary or leaving. They also told me if I stayed with the show, I would not be allowed to work as a news reporter in the newsroom because of potential conflict of interest with clients who were now paying to be on television. If I left the show, I could continue working as a full-time news reporter, but my managers couldn't tell me what my new schedule would be. Would I work mornings? Nights? Weekends? The morning show had given me the balance I needed as a single parent to continuing working and to be there for my son. I had a Monday through Friday nine-to-five-thirty schedule, and I wanted to know if that was going to change, but management could not give me a definitive answer.

Jared was twelve, almost thirteen years old. He was about to become a teenager entering middle school. This was going to be a huge transition in his life, and all the more reason why I wanted to know what my work schedule would be. I continued to inquire but, again and again, received no definitive answer. All that station management could tell me was that if I left the show, I would be reporting in the newsroom, and even though they couldn't specify a schedule in advance of me signing the new contract they offered, they told me there would be *no* anchoring opportunities for me at the station anymore—which meant instead of set hours working in the studio as I had before, I would have unpredictable hours working in the field as a news reporter. That could mean anything. Early mornings. Late nights. Weekends. Holidays. And the truth of the matter was, after thirteen years with the station, and some twenty years in the business, I had been there, done that. It just wasn't fun anymore.

109

The upside, and there was one, was that for nearly all of my adult life, I had a forum to tell stories, which is all I had ever wanted to do. It just so happened I told stories on television because of an inherited gift of gab and telegenic looks I have my parents to thank for. My love of writing and my ability to translate my curiosity into questions that people seemed to want to answer had all worked in my favor. People liked seeing me on television, and I liked being on it.

I had gotten to cover numerous plum assignments over the years, everything from a national political convention to flying in helicopters, riding on the now decommissioned USS Dwight D. Eisenhower aircraft carrier. There was the assignment that sent me off to follow the trek of the monarch butterfly from Minnesota to Mexico; I swam with dolphins in the Bahamas as part of another theme-park feature. There was the stress-inducing interview with Jay Leno backstage at *The Tonight Show*, and even an in-studio interview with Sarah Ferguson the Duchess of York, and a cooking segment with Martha Stewart during which I baked the cover cake from one of her cookbooks. The cook in me is still proud of the fact that the nation's top homemaking maven tasted my cake and said it was good.

Probably one of the biggest plum assignments was when I traveled to London to interview Victoria Beckham and the Spice Girls. At the time the group had sold 32 million records worldwide and had hired Minneapolis duo Jimmy Jam Harris and Terri Lewis to produce songs for their next album. Jimmy and Terry had one hundred gold and platinum hits to their name at the time and I had interviewed them several times over the years, which led to me snagging this overseas assignment. Jimmy Jam, as we called him, was the more talkative of the two, a big, extremely well-spoken teddy bear of a man who was often described as someone who reminded you of your favorite uncle. Terry Lewis, on the other hand, with his chiseled jawline and quiet eyes, was equally brilliant, yet nonetheless more elusive and quiet. Whenever I was at their Flyte Tyme recording studios, I never knew for sure if Lewis was going to be there. Sometimes I'd see him, most of the time I didn't, which lead me to nickname him "The Phantom."

Jimmy and Terry were so in demand at the time that artists flew to Minneapolis from places like L.A. and London just to record with them at their studio. This would be the first time Jimmy and Terry would travel across the pond to work with a group. They would record two songs in four days with the Spice Girls—Scary, Posh, Baby, and Sporty—at the legendary Whitfield Street recording studios in central London.

It was surreal being behind the scenes of a pop group that at the time was one of the biggest groups in the world. Myself and a station photographer named Jeff had complete access inside the studio, watching and filming as the Spice Girls, chewing wads of bubble gum, clad in sweat pants and skimpy tank tops, would scribble and then cross out lyrics on a sheet of paper with a pencil, confer with Jimmy and Terry who would play chords of music on the keyboards, then once they all agreed on something, immediately head back into the recording studio to lay down vocals. I was there for a day-long studio session and watched as they recorded the song "Oxygen." Between takes I'd interview them and they couldn't have been nicer—friendly, funny, loved the camera, and had lots of good things to say about Jimmy and Terry.

The producing duo were also responsible for me getting the chance to chat it up with pop star Mariah Carey a few times during her stops in Minneapolis. Jimmy and Terry were producing Mariah's newest album at Flyte Tyme studios, and Mariah had come to town to record a music video at a huge outdoor summer music festival at Canterbury Downs in Shakopee. Photographer Jeff and I had been told by the festival media director that if we wanted an interview with Mariah Carey, we had to be in the park by 9:30 a.m. at the latest. We got there on time, and then waited and waited. As one band after another took to the stage, we kept waiting. With no sign of Mariah, we just waited and waited. The media director kept telling us to sit tight, but couldn't confirm one way or the other if we were going to get the interview. And so we waited all day long.

Finally, late into the afternoon and early evening, Mariah Carey appeared on stage and the crowd roared. Jeff and I were in the crowd filming. After her performance, we were taken by golf carts deep into the woods. The sun had set and all the festival's media director had told us was to get in the cart and not ask any questions. Mariah was nowhere in sight. Not knowing where we were being taken or why we were being taken there felt a little bit like being in a summer horror flick. You know the scene where the unsuspecting victims are wandering aimlessly in the woods right before something really bad happens? Well, yeah, that's what it looked like and felt like to me.

I was exhausted, we had waited all day and had still not gotten an interview with Mariah, and now we were riding deeper and deeper into the woods. Suddenly we came to a clearing where there were lots of bright lights, parked trailers, and people milling about. I then realized we had been driven to the secret location of Mariah's music video set. It was a pretty amazing sight. Mariah emerged from one of the trailers wearing the same itsy-bitsy army green crocheted deep v-neck halter top she had performed in. She had added a tiny matching cashmere sweater over it, but my hand was still shaking as I attached the lapel microphone to the left side of her sweater. We sat side by side on tall director's chairs and once the camera was rolling she talked about how she had had the chorus to the song "Thank God I Found You" in her head for months and she knew Jimmy Jam and Terry Lewis were the guys to help her write and record the song.

Jimmy and Terry, she said, had a reputation for being the best in music business when it comes to tailor-making songs to fit a recording artist's particular style. She told me she considered them the best in the business and had flown all the way to Minneapolis for a chance to work with them. After the interview, Jimmy Jam, who had been watching quietly off to the side, invited Jeff and me back to Flyte Tyme studios where Mariah and pop boy band 98 Degrees would be recording music until 2:00 a.m. It was as up-close and personal as it gets. We had full behind-the-scenes access. We ran between sound booths and recording sessions shooting video and interviewing various members of the band and Mariah's entourage for a story that would run during the station's ratings period. I got home at 4:00 a.m.

As big a "get" as that story was, I'll never forget what Jimmy Jam Harris, a husband and father and native Minnesotan, told me during an interview. He was at the top of his game. He and Terry Lewis had a line of A-list pop stars, like jet liners lining up on a runway, waiting to work with them, clients who were willing to leave the comforts of LA and come to Minneapolis to record because this duo were proven hit makers. In 1986 they won a Grammy for Producers of the Year, and years later would be inducted into the Songwriters Hall of Fame. Even with all of their success, Jimmy told me their appeal was about something more.

"[The artists] see hard work and clean living," Jimmy Jam said, "which is kind of a misnomer in terms of the recording business. People think of it as not a family thing, you know sort of a sordid drug-filled whatever. But then you walk into a building like this and you see just a couple of guys from Minneapolis that work hard and live clean, you see what can happen."

"A couple of guys from Minneapolis, that work hard and live clean…." That's how Jimmy Jam described himself and that left a great impression on me. As a news reporter I had seen and been exposed to my fair share of things—not all of them pretty. I had no problem with working hard, but in all honesty, living clean was a struggle. To me that meant steering clear of vices like drugs and alcohol, which at times was hard because it was so pervasive in the news business. It seemed everybody drank and I was odd because I didn't. Yet, after my interview with Jimmy Jam Harris, a self-described teetotaler, I didn't feel that odd anymore.

As a feature reporter I covered music and even sports. I had covered every major sports team in Minnesota, and there I was again, this time down on the field inside the now-demolished Hubert H. Humphrey Metrodome, during the Minnesota Vikings' colossal, storied, and heartbreaking loss to the Atlanta Falcons during the 1998 NFC championship game. I had covered the Vikings all season long, writing sidebars and feature stories about what the team was doing off the field, while leaving game stats and division rankings to the more capable sports reporters. I had gotten an exclusive interview with Minnesota Vikings coach Dennis Green at his home with his second wife, Marie, and their two children.

They lived in a stately historic home in a prestigious Minneapolis neighborhood near Lake Harriet. Marie had added contemporary accents to the inside of the house and we set up for the interview in their living room. I remember seeing a side of the man that few people got to see. He was a father, a husband, and a man of faith. During the interview, Coach Green stated his priorities on camera: faith, family, and football, in that order.

Under Coach Dennis Green the team had implemented Community Tuesdays. Every Tuesday, Vikings' players would go out to schools and talk to kids, volunteer at food kitchens, or hold clothing drives—and the media would follow. The station had assigned me to cover those community events, so when the team went 16–1, and were heavy favorites heading into the NFC championship game against the Atlanta Falcons, my assignment was to get fan reaction. The hope of course was for a win and a Super Bowl appearance. I was excited about the possibility of covering my first Super Bowl. It was a career goal of mine and now I was one game away from it becoming a reality. Yet in the back of my mind, I thought how devastating it would be if the team didn't win. It seemed no one thought the Vikings could lose. It had been a magical, unprecedented season and everyone in town just *knew* the Minnesota Vikings were headed to the Super Bowl that year. The television station had already ordered custom Super Bowl news team T-shirts and built a miniature news desk that would be shipped down to Miami and used during all of our Super Bowl newscasts. It was a done deal in everyone's mind. They just had to win. How could it not be? The team was 16–1, NFC conference champs, and kicker Gary Anderson hadn't missed a field goal all season.

I had interviewed Anderson during the season after Jared had asked me why his helmet was so funny looking. That was one of the really cool things about my job; if I wanted to know something, I could go find out and tell people about it. So I pitched the question of Gary's Anderson's helmet in the morning editorial meeting, and news managers liked the idea. I called the Vikings' public relations manager, and a few hours later, I was sitting in front of Minnesota Vikings' kicker Gary Anderson, camera rolling, asking why his helmet was so goofy looking. The answer? It was the first one he had ever been issued by the NFL, he liked it, and he saw no reason to change. I went home that night and Jared got the answer to his question when he saw his mom's story on the 5:00 p.m. news. He thought that was pretty cool.

116

Who would have imagined that, later in the season, it would come down to a missed field goal by that same Gary Anderson? The Minnesota Vikings had taken an early lead 20–7 as quarterback Randall Cunningham threw and ran for two touchdowns by the end of the second quarter. The score was 27–17 Vikings by the end of third quarter. By the last 10 minutes of the fourth quarter the score was 27–20. I was standing on the sidelines behind the team bench. The anxiety was palpable. I could feel it. My heart was pounding through my chest as I watched Vikings' players, massive and sweaty, anxiously pacing back and forth on the sidelines. Coaches glanced at the clock, talked into headsets, and conferred with each other. Coach Green was steady like a rock. There were two minutes left in the game and a field goal would have sealed the deal. I almost couldn't stand the pressure. I had never felt anything like it. We got word from the station that we, the photojournalist and I, needed to be up on the concourse to grab fan reaction as soon as the game ended, so we headed back up to the satellite truck parked just outside the stadium. I was actually relieved not to be down on the field for the end of the game. I sat in the truck and watched on the tiny screen as Gary Anderson missed a 38-yard field goal attempt that would have sealed a Vikings victory. Instead, the Atlanta Falcons tied the game 27–27 with a touchdown, sending it into overtime. Atlanta went on to break Minnesota's heart, winning the game 30–27, with, ironically, a 38-yard field goal.

The Metrodome, which had been ear-piercingly loud and rau-cous, fell silent. Sixty-four thousand fans were in utter disbelief. As they slowly made their way out of the stadium and onto the concourse, I remember the only sound was the feet shuffling of silent, broken-hearted fans. I couldn't get an interview. No one wanted to talk to me. People just kept passing me by. I spotted some of the player's wives, whom I knew, and all they said was "not now." They were too devastated to talk. To this day, my heart still beats through my chest when I think about that day and how close the Vikings came to winning it all.

After ten seasons with the Vikings, Coach Green and his family eventually left Minnesota to take coaching positions elsewhere. Years later, on July 22, 2016, the Minnesota Vikings opened the new billion-dollar US Bank Stadium on the sight of the old Metrodome. Coach Dennis Green had died from a heart attack at age 67 just the day before.

God rest his soul.

The year following the Vikings' devastating play-off loss, I found myself in the middle of another huge event, fueled by yet another Minnesota icon. The year was 1999 and Minneapolis music superstar Prince was throwing a New Year's Eve party. He billed his "Rave un2 the Year 2000" as the last time he would ever sing his hit song "1999," which he had written in 1982. The song would be played at New Year's Eve parties around world. A few weeks before New Year's Eve, Prince was throwing his own party at his famous Paisley Park studios, which would be filmed and edited into a MTV pay-per-view special that would be seen worldwide.

118

Prince issued purple numbered tickets stamped in brass. It was *the* ticket to have in Minneapolis that year, and I had one. By some strange turn of events, I found myself on the VIP list of the biggest party of the year at the turn of the new millennium. The only piece of Prince memorabilia I still own is the brass ticket I used to gain entry that night.

There I was in the deep purple-hued halls of Chanhassen's Paisley Park with the likes of rock stars Lenny Kravitz, Morris Day of the Time, Larry Graham; television stars Lisa Ling and Star Jones; and a whole squadron of Minnesota Vikings, plus hundreds of invited fans and party guests.

It was standing room only inside Prince's massive sound stage, where a huge lighted sign of his trademark symbol hung from back of the elevated stage. A live band was positioned on tiers on stage and muscular, six-foot tall bodyguards in tight white t-shirts and black suits were everywhere.

Prince would perform with the band and various artists, then disappear and reappear in a different monochromatic outfit. He wore a long-sleeved turquoise lamé top and matching pants when he rocked out with Lenny Kravitz on "American Woman." Lenny Kravitz wore sunglasses, rust-colored leather pants, and a matching leather jacket. They entered from the back of the crowd with their guitars strapped on, flanked by half a dozen bodyguards who formed a human barrier keeping the crush of frenzied fans at bay as Prince and Kravitz made their way up to the stage.

I was off to one side on a roped-off elevated platform reserved for the VIP guests. I remember thinking how incredible this was—the music, Paisley Park, Prince, the band, the celebrities, the cameras and producers, and watching the behind-the-scenes machinations of what went into to producing a television special event of this caliber and scale. The director told the crowd when to cheer and clap, when to be still, and where to look. Between musical numbers there was lots of standing around and long periods of waiting while the cameras repositioned. The crowd stood and chatted with each other as they waited for the next act to take the stage.

I remember watching how the director orchestrated Prince jumping into a mosh pit to make it look like it was totally spontaneous, when in reality the whole thing had been carefully choreographed with multiple bodyguards hidden in the crowd to make sure the scene went as planned. Prince was passed through the crowd on his back and placed on a platform with his piano, where he launched into the next song.

At one point during the night, Prince reappeared wearing another monochromatic outfit, this time deep purple. Standing behind him on stage, dressed in all black, was a local gospel choir. Prince stepped to the microphone, guitar in hand, and launched into an impassioned performance of a song called "The Christ" as the choir sang backup. That number transformed the party into the type of spiritual celebration I had experienced countless times during my life on Sunday morning. That was the thing about Prince—he was a worldly and often times controversial musical genius, who was also deeply spiritual.

120

At the end of the night, by now the early hours of the morning, after an amazing set list that ranged from gospel to rock to hip hop and everything in between, the moment everyone had been waiting for finally came. Prince reappeared, this time, wearing silver lamé, including a silver kerchief wrapped around his long black hair. He asked the crowd whether we were ready, taunting and teasing us, counting down into his microphone until the familiar chord strains of "1999" sent the crowd into another frenzy.

It was surreal. Then, something even more amazing happened. One of Prince's bodyguards came over to the area where I was standing and took down the velvet rope that separated the VIP platform from the stage and *waved us all on stage with Prince!* Purple balloons fell from the ceiling, then a blizzard of silver confetti, and more balloons, and I remember all the while standing in the back of the people on stage watching all of it. It felt like I was in a dream. I inched my way up through all the people who were dancing around on stage until at one point, toward the end of the song as the last few flecks of confetti fell, I found myself standing center stage right next to Prince. He was so tiny! He looked at me. I looked at him. My first instinct was to grab him and give him a big hug. But I remembered all those huge bodyguards lurking about. I had heard stories of how swiftly Prince's security team would usher people out the door for even the slightest infraction, so I decided against hugging him. I extended my hand instead. He took it, shook it, looked me dead in the eye, smiled that wry smile of his, then turned and walked up a lighted staircase and vanished for the night.

Years later, when Prince died at age fifty-seven in April of 2016, I remembered my brief encounter with him, an international superstar, with his bespoke clothing and golden tickets, part Willy Wonka and part Peter Pan all rolled into one. His death became international wall-to-wall breaking news. The network crews rolled into town with their A-list talent, and stayed for days on end before they all packed up and left. There were lighted billboards and impromptu hand-painted street murals. Bridges were awash in lavender light. The Twin Cities' sadness at the passing of its native star was compounded by the weather. It rained in Minneapolis for days after Prince died. The makeshift memorials at Prince's palatial Paisley Park in suburban Chanhassen and at First Avenue in downtown Minneapolis where his iconic movie "Purple Rain" was filmed, grew daily with soggy and rain-soaked flowers and placards. Yet amid the dreary forecasts and broken hearts there were even more parties and street dances. Prince's memory had brought

121

Minnesotans together. He had put us on the map and now he was gone. For all of Prince Rogers Nelson's fame and notoriety, now that he was gone, I hoped, or rather prayed, the words one of my church mothers growing up used to say when someone left this earth: "Baby, I sure do hope he don't have no trouble at the river"; meaning, of course, that for all of his earthly accomplishments, let's hope he was heaven-bound and his soul made it to the other side.

Prince, Mariah Carey, the Spice Girls, butterflies in Mexico, and Jay Leno in California—those kinds of experiences came along with the sort of assignments that now belonged to the pre-Internet era of broadcast news, when local television stations ruled with big budgets and huge advertising revenues that paid for the air travel and hotels, expensive talent and high-profile stories. Not anymore. The well had dried up. Travel, especially for fluffy feature stories, was a thing of the past, deemed too costly and inconsequential to justify the expense.

I had once clipped a little quote from an issue of *Oprah* magazine and framed it. It said: *Never move backward. Side to side, diagonally, up and down, but never backward.* I had placed it on my bathroom vanity. I looked at that quote every single morning, and as I began to contemplate my future with the station, I knew I didn't want to go backward. After a combined twenty years in the television news business, hopping from market to market until I landed back home in Minneapolis, I had covered every kind of story and done just about every kind of interview, to the point where news reporting

122

was no longer that much of a challenge. I had had my fill of knocking on the doors of dead people's relatives and asking them, "How do you feel?" I had been given press releases and newspaper clippings at nine in the morning and been told to make a story out them by five in the evening—hundreds of times. I had interviewed the same officials about the same controversies and gotten the same sound bites over and over again. Was the expiration of my contract my way out?

I remember very vividly the day I made my decision. It was evening and I was at home. My son was sleeping upstairs in his room. I was sitting alone in the dark at my living room table, drinking a cup of chamomile tea. I was physically tired and mentally exhausted with the weight of the decision in front of me. Stay or go? Stay or go? Single moms with mortgages don't quit their jobs. But quiet as it's kept, being on television is a very stressful profession: having to be perfectly groomed and well-spoken on live television every day; the pressure to perform; the competition; and now, added on top of all of that, television stations that at one time seemed to have a license to print money were unstable, volatile, in unfamiliar territory.

So there, sitting at my dining room table in the dark, in my tiny little house all by myself, while my son slept upstairs, I prayed. I asked God to show me the way. If I stayed with the infotainment pay-to-play show, how would that impact my career as a journalist? What would my schedule be? If I left the show and returned to the newsroom full time, who would be there for my son if I were called out on a story late at night or early in the morning? Would I be able to go to his teacher conferences? His games? Would we

123

still be able to have family dinner? What would transitioning to a teenager be like for him? Would I be able to be there as a parent to help him find his way? How would I pay my bills? Oh, my head was swirling. I had drawn a line down the center of a notepad and written down the pros and cons on each side. I had talked with my family and friends and other people in the industry, but in the end the decision was mine. So I prayed.

God, please, what am I to do?

I put my head down on the dining room table out of exhaustion, and that's when I heard it.

Resign.

124   Plain as day I heard the word.

Resign.

I lifted up my head, and immediately a peace came over me. I actually felt a sense of relief. I crawled into bed that night with a smile on my face, and for the first time in a long time, slept.

A few weeks later, I was at church and a guest minister, Pastor Gary McIntosh, was delivering the Sunday morning message. I had never seen this man before in my life. He was preaching away, and all of a sudden he stopped in the middle of his sermon and said he felt the need to pray. This was very, very unusual for our church.

I was sitting off to one side in the front row, and when Pastor McIntosh called for the congregation to stand, I stood. When he said, "Let's pray," I prayed. The entire congregation started praying very loudly. In all my years of attending church, I had never quite experienced something like this.

Then the pastor walked from around the pulpit and stood directly in front of the congregation. People were praying, and now some had started weeping. It was a real spiritual outpouring taking place. It was in that atmosphere that Pastor McIntosh said the words that have stayed with me from that day to this:

"You are free to be who God made you to be, and God will be with you."

Oh my goodness. When he said that, I felt like he was talking directly to me.

You are free to be who God made you to be, and God will be with you.

Something inside of me broke. All the anxiety and pressure and confusion and frustration over the decision before me came flooding to the surface, spilling out in front of everyone right there in the front row. I began to weep. Then cry. Then sob. I sobbed and sobbed and sobbed. Right there in the front row. People were huddled around me, patting my back, holding my hand, and I just cried and cried and cried. The ushers kept handing me one tissue after another. I must have gone through a whole box. I just cried. And when I was done crying, I knew I was free.

I didn't know what my future was going to be like, but on the inside I knew that the time had come for me to transition, and God would be with me all of the way. I can't explain it. I just knew it. After the service that day, I went home and wrote my letter of resignation.

It wasn't easy walking away from a career I had dreamed about and pursued from the time I was eleven years old. I had lots of sleepless nights and tears and prayers and counseling about what I should do next. I was a single mom with a mortgage. How could I just walk away?

Little did I know I just missed a huge tidal wave that was about to hit the broadcasting industry nationwide. The following year, in 2007, the country went into a deep recession and television stations around the country began slashing budgets and laying off staff like I had never seen before. No one, it seemed, was spared. Veteran star anchors with long tenures and even longer paycheck stubs were being let go. It was a scary time to be in local television news.

I had paid down my debt and tucked away my nickels. My church offered me a freelance gig producing in-house videos, and I found another small freelance gig as a blogger for *MinnPost*, an online newspaper that had just launched and was hiring veteran journalists like me. The editors asked me to write a piece about how the broadcasting industry had been adversely affected in the wake of the recession. I still had several contacts at television stations around the city, and I called them for help with the story, which ended up being one of the most widely read pieces published on the *MinnPost* site that year. Here's an excerpt:

> You know you've lived awhile when what seems implausible happens. Those of us in local television who were lucky enough to ascend to a prime-time anchor spot on the evening

news used to work under the illusion of immunity. Barring any sort of public scandal or ratings decline, we were, as *American Idol*'s Ryan Seacrest might say, safe. Anchors, after all, were the face of a station, personalities who had earned the public trust—which resulted in ratings, which of course translated into revenue. Losing a star anchor meant risking a ratings decline, so whatever cuts had to be made remained, for the most part, hidden from public view.

Not anymore.

In a series of shock waves, stations across the country responded to declining revenues and viewers bore witness to long-time, popular, six- and seven-figure news reporters and anchors being shown the door...in droves. In L.A. San Francisco. Sacramento. New York. Denver. Dallas. Pittsburgh. Philadelphia. Chicago. Boston. And Minneapolis.

Looking back at it now, I'm grateful I was able to leave on my own terms, rather than be unceremoniously shown the door like many of my former colleagues had to experience. Quitting my job was anything but easy. It was one of the most difficult decisions I've ever made in my life. And it was also the beginning of a huge transformative journey.

Even to this day, looking back on my decision to walk away from my television news career, there was never any doubt in my mind it was the right decision. If I had it to do all over again, I would make the same decision.

8

FULLNESS OF JOY

You will show me the path of life; in Your presence there is
fullness of joy; at Your right hand are pleasures forevermore.
—Psalm 16:11

God said He would never leave us or forsake us.[3] That day in church, when the floodgates broke and the tears fell, He also told me I was free. Free to be who He made me to be, and that He would be right there beside me every step of the way. Through every lonely moment and difficult decision.

Next to my divorce, walking away from my career was the hardest thing I had ever done in my life. It was a time of great uncertainty, self-doubt, insecurity, restlessness, anxiety, and a depressing sense of loss.

The first few weeks after I quit my job, I would sit in my living room playing Scrabble on my computer. After all, I was a professional journalist, a wordsmith. Words were my lifeblood. My biggest fear was that my brain would turn to mush. So I played Scrabble until it was time to pick my son up from school. Then I would make him a snack, and while he watched cartoons, I took a nap. Those naps were some of the deepest most satisfying sleep I had experienced in years.

Deep, peaceful, restful, satisfying, and restorative sleep. I could just feel the stress sloughing off and melting away.

Even though I was restless, strangely enough, my sleep was restful. I looked forward to those naps, because at the beginning stages of this new phase of my life, those naps were the only time I felt at peace.

Most of the time, I felt confusion. I didn't know who I was anymore. For nearly twenty years people had associated me with a variety of different station call letters. I was, or had been, "that lady on TV" for more than two decades. That's how people related to me. Even my own parents.

"You're making quite a name for the family there, girl," my father would say.

And my mother, God bless my mother. I think she watched every minute of every hour of every day that I was on television. It never failed: at some point and time during my workweek I would walk out of the studio and back to my desk and the message light on my phone would be on. It would always be her. Mom. And it would always be some variation of the same voice mail message: "Hey there, pretty girl," would be her standard beginning. "You looked so pretty today on the air today," she would say. "What's that you were wearing? It looked like a blue on my television."

Or red, or orange, or black. She never quite trusted the color setting on her television to deliver the truth.

"Have I seen that before?" she would ask, referring to the particular ensemble I wore on the air that day. I can't be certain, but at times I suspected one of the main reasons she tuned everyday was just to see what I was wearing.

"Girl, where do you put all those clothes?"

And she'd continue, "I didn't want anything, I'm just calling to let you know I was watching today, well I actually watch every day...what was that you all were cooking? Some sort of shrimp? I can't eat seafood with my allergies and all, it would set my nose to running something scandalous. But it sure did look good. Well anyway, pretty girl, I was just calling to tell you I love you so much, and I am so proud of you. You don't have to call me back, I actually have to run out of here to the post office, and then I have an appointment down town today with Dr. Bloomingthal. I tell you, these allergies...but I'm not going to complain. Okay, pretty girl...I love you. This is Mom. Bye."

If she had left one, she had left a hundred of those messages. I would save them, for weeks on end. And now there was no reason for her to call me at work anymore.

My parents still lived in the same house I grew up in, in Roseville, a small suburb of St. Paul. And when I and my four brothers, and their wives and children, would gather at my parent's house for Thanksgiving and Christmas, it was always the same conversation: "Hey Sis, saw that story you did on the Timberwolves. You think you can hook me up with some tickets?"

People were always, always asking for a hook up. Because you see, as a television personality, I was considered one of the beautiful people in town. (The local gossip columnists actually wrote once that I was a "fixture" at events where all the beautiful people could be found.) Being on television every day meant I had social currency; VIP passes, front row seats, theatrical debuts, restaurant openings, and party invitations were a regular part of my existence.

Because I was on live TV for an hour a day, five days week, public relations reps wanted me to read their client's book, see their client's show, wear their client's clothes, eat their client's food, shop at their client's store with the hopes that I would talk about it on television, which equated to loads of free publicity. That's how the game was, and in many ways is still, played. A game where everybody, PR flacks, their clients, and TV personalities all benefit. It was a very privileged life.

And I had chosen to walk away from it all.

131

It didn't take very long at all for me to realize that without a celebrity association, people just didn't know what to say to me anymore. There were awkward encounters at the grocery store. People who used to ask me about the weather, or the last news story, or station gossip, simply didn't know what to say to me anymore. They were so used to relating to me because of what I did versus relating to me simply because of who I was.

The invitations to restaurant openings and parties stopped coming. Press passes and VIP perks all dried up. The privileges of a celebrity life slowly began to fade away, and I was laid bare to face who I was without them.

What happens to us when the safety net is no longer there? What happens when the routine of going to the same place at the same time, performing the same function with the same people, evaporates? When the safety of similarity and predictability vanishes? When the routines that tell us, albeit superficially, that we're doing okay—go away? What happens when that covering is removed? I know what happens, because I lived it: we are laid bare, exposed, and broken, left to confront who we really are. That's what happened to me.

In the first few months after I resigned from my job, I remember sitting in a Starbucks at nine o'clock in the morning after I had dropped my son off from school. I had no place to go and nothing to do. It was first time in over two decades that I could actually have coffee at nine o'clock in the morning. During my news reporting career, I was always in an editorial meeting at 9:00 a.m. I remember thinking about my former life—story ideas and deadlines—and my current reality—sweatpants and lattes. Just when I was about to start to feel sorry for myself, I looked over at the table next to me and saw an elderly woman and a little girl, I presumed grandmother and granddaughter.

The grandmother, with one eye on her granddaughter, was up at the counter ordering coffee and apple juice while the little girl waited patiently at a table. The little girl wearing a lavender coat, patterned tights, and Mary-Janes, had big brown eyes, and her long brown hair was pulled back in a wispy ponytail. Just as I glanced over at her, the little girl caught my eye, and smiled at me. She smiled at me, and in doing so, that sweet innocent child gave me a gift—a tiny, innocent pocket of joy. Her sweet face melted my heart and I thought to myself how fortunate I was. I realized that if I had been in that 9:00 a.m. editorial meeting, I would have missed her smile.

It hit me at that moment how tightly wound I had been all these years—*go, go, go get the story, make the deadline, beat the competition.* Go. Go, and go. And when you're done going, go again, because as they said in the news business, you're only as good as your last story. I wondered how many moments like the moment I just had, I had missed. Did that little girl know I use to be on TV? I doubt it. She wasn't smiling at me because I was on TV, she was smiling at me because I was *me.* An innocent and brief exchange at nine in the morning that I'll never forgot. I thought about what I used to be doing and what I was doing now; I was slowing down. I was being me. I was now free to be me.

For so much of my life, I had mistakenly believed my value as a person was determined by my professional title, status, and achievement. "News reporter." "News anchor." "Talk show-host." "Celebrity." Without those titles I felt I was nothing. I felt like a failure, a loser. I continued to believe that my value as a human being rested solely in the title I possessed as a professional, until I slowly began to realize that simply was not, and was never, true… in the bigger scheme of things.

133

One day my friend Kim met me for coffee and gave me a book written by journalist Maria Shriver titled *Just Who Will You Be?* Shriver writes about how hard it was for her to step down from her correspondent job at NBC news when she became the First Lady of the state of California. I read that book from cover to cover in one sitting and slept with it on my nightstand for months. It was that book that helped me begin to transition from who I use to be to who I really am. In her book, Maria Shriver, someone with fame and legacy, wrote: "Fame in and of itself can't make you happy. It can't make you feel worthy. It can't give you a life of meaning and joy. That, I've learned, is strictly an inside job."[4]

Those words struck me at my very core. I realized I had been successful as a television news personality not because somebody gave me a title, but because of certain abilities and talents that I possessed innately. Being able to write and speak publicly are the things that got me the titles. And even though the external titles were now gone, those innate, God-given abilities that I had worked my tail off to hone and perfect, were still there, and no one could ever take them away from me. They could take the title. But they could never take my talent.

134

Maria Shriver wrote in her book how she had discovered a new sense of self, and a new, more fulfilling life, outside of broadcast news. And so did I. I had discovered a life where sharing who you authentically are with family and close friends brings a warmth and authentic intimacy to everyday life. A life where knowing who you are from the inside out gives you the courage to draw a line in the sand, and state confidently: This is who I am, and this is what I stand for. This is the person I have worked so hard to become; this is what matters to me; this is where my priorities lie; this is what I care about. And while my position or status may change, shifts in social constructs have no bearing on who I am on the inside.

I knew that if I were ever going to be truly happy in life and experience the joy that comes from knowing who you are, then I had to decide. I had to choose to believe in who I am from the inside out.

I had to choose to be free.

PART II:
THE JOY

Introduction

SEVEN STEPS TO JOY

You will live in joy and peace.
—Isaiah 55:12 NLT

Happiness is what we all want. It's why we get up and go to work, and why we work so hard and so long. It's why we save and sacrifice. It's why we give and give and give some more. We do it because we think there's a big payoff at the end. We think *this time* I'll be happy. *This time* I'll find the pot of gold. *This time* is my time.

Yet when the payoff doesn't pay out, when our hopes have been dashed, and when our projected delight turns to protracted disappointment, what do we do? Sulk, anesthetize, shift, redirect, change partners, plans, and projects, and start all over again—give and give and give; work, work, work; seek, hope, and pray that maybe this time, THIS time; *maybe, just maybe, this time I'll be happy.* Once we land the job, get the guy or the girl, buy the house, or get that new designer handbag or expensive watch, then we'll be happy.

Might I humbly suggest that happiness is not the pot at the end of a rainbow?

Happiness and joy are not final destinations like some stops on the Green Line. Happiness isn't a hidden treasure. Happiness isn't what someone "makes" you, or something you "get," because there will always be more and bigger and better stuff to make and get. Chasing happiness that way is a pursuit that never ends. You'll end up looking like a hamster running frantically on its wheel.

Happiness, I believe, has little do with external acquisitions and is more like a gentle river's current; an internal force flowing through our lives; a current that we can choose to tap into at any time, because the river flows continuously. Happiness is a *state of being* and that state is called *joy.*

If there is one point I want to get across in these pages, it's this: as we persevere along life's journey, we must be intentional about looking for and finding joy. It's not *life* that fails to produce joy; it's *we* who fail to recognize it. If you find yourself saying, "someday I'll be happy," well, today can be your someday. Joy is all around us, and we have the choice to engage in the process—to embark upon a pathway that produces joy along the way. In Part I, I shared my many pockets of joy. I could say these moments were really small miracles that happened spontaneously, and that I stopped to recognize them.

But there is something more. I believe, with a little practice and lots of intentionality, we can *all* create joy in our lives. I spent a lot of time reading about happiness, and now I want to join the conversation of just how happiness works its way into our everyday. You've read my story and know *my* path; now I want to focus on *your* path. I want talk about very specific ways you can create joy in your life. Your story may be different from mine, but I believe there are pathways to joy we can all follow. We all have the potential to possess moments of joy at any time, however big or small.

138

Being intentional about looking for joy in life is a lot like good table manners; it requires that we slow down, give thanks, and pay attention to what we are about to partake. Most of the time, what's in front of us comes in small, bite-sized pieces, which over time add up to be something quiet memorable and satisfying. If we follow the right "recipe" and are intentional about crafting happy "dining experiences," we can absolutely create those moments of joy. The key word here is *intentionality*. We must look for joy on purpose.

Why is it that the only time we marvel at sunrises and sunsets is on vacation? I know, I know. The day's impressive beginning and end happen every day yet we're too busy to take note. Or why are we oblivious to the sound of the soothing patter of rainfall? Because we are hurriedly trying to avoid it as we make our way from point A to point B. The wind makes no sound as it moves through the trees because we don't stop, however briefly, just to listen. Listen to our own breathing and heartbeat, the miracles that they are. Listen to the gleeful sing-song chatter of a toddler busy at play or the contented panting of a tail-wagging dog during our morning walk.

And you know what else we don't listen to? Our heart's desire. It gets drowned out by that pesky critter known as "expectation" and its equally onerous second cousin "perception." We're so occupied being and doing what we think we're supposed to that we don't take the time to listen—to be who and to do what we really want. We put our hopes and dreams on mute and we miss it. We miss our life. We miss those pockets of joy.

I truly believe happiness is a choice.[5] We can choose to be happy; we can choose to be intentional about looking for and finding the

139

joy in our life; we can choose to make a conscious effort to see the glass half-full instead of half-empty. As you've seen, all of my life I have been annoyingly optimistic. I said this once to a podcast host during an interview, and she replied, "But Roxane, optimism is also contagious!" I think she's right. It all starts with intentionality.

And as you will see in the pages ahead, experiencing more joy in our lives will, at times, not only require intentionality, but also courage. After growing up with four brothers, I know a little about courage. From the time I stuck my hand down a hole in the back yard to see what was there, to flying cross-country by myself, to training for marathons and mud races and refusing to quit, to walking away from that which, despite my best efforts, just wasn't working, my family has always said I had guts—an ability to wonder and then proceed to find out what lies beyond the hurt and fear.

It's clear to me now that optimism drives courage. Think about it—what if we were brave enough to be courageously happy? What if we were brave enough, in spite of what life throws at us, to do the heavy lifting, to place the pavers and set the stones on a path that not only leads to happiness, but produces pockets of joy along the way? Rather than longing for some far-off, problem-free destination, what if, smack dab in the middle of our mess and life's imperfections, we could see the joy that is set before us?

Imagine paving a path of markers and moments where you chose to see the joy, be it in tiny increments or big sloppy splashes. Imagine looking back and seeing the work that you've done. Then

140

imagine standing on the pathway you've created and looking forward with the knowledge you can continue to pave a path, step by step, that reflects joy.

And so here in Part II are seven concrete steps you can take to find the pockets of joy along your life's journey. This list is by no means exhaustive, but it is deeply personal. I've put the following chapters together using examples from my own life; joyful experiences that I've supported with stories and research. My hope is that this work will inspire you to make the decision to see the joy that is set before us each and every day.[6]

9

AUTHENTICITY

*A twinkle in the eye means joy in the heart,
and good news makes you feel fit as a fiddle.*
—Proverbs 15:30 MSG

W̲ho are you? What makes you tick? When you feel the happiest, where are you and what are you doing? Who are you with?

Why am I asking so many questions? Because these questions
will help you identify your true, authentic self. No one likes a phony,
because it's hard to trust a person when you don't know who they are
or what they stand for. I read once that this is the reason why some
people have a fear of circus clowns; their comical, heavily made-up
faces conceal their true intent. It's a matter of trust, or lack thereof.

The happiest moments in our lives are the moments when we
are being true to ourselves, and admittedly, that can be hard to do
when there are so many societal standards and expectations to live
up to—believe me, I know this firsthand. During my television
news career, the pressure to be thin and beautiful bore down on
me with every appearance in front of a lens.

I remember being on assignment in Orlando in 2000 when
Disney World threw a huge turn-of-the-century party. Over the

years I had taken multiple trips to Orlando to cover new attractions at the theme parks there, but this public relations party was unlike anything I had ever seen, before or since. Disney's Magic Kingdom closed to the general public and dressed up for the media and "special invited guests." Three thousand of them. My co-host, Pat, and I were part of the on-air crew the station had sent down from Minneapolis to cover it all. As we entered the park, we were greeted almost immediately by waitrons dressed in black and white, carrying trays of clear plastic martini glasses filled with a murky pink concoction I had come to recognize as cosmopolitans. Vodka with a splash of cranberry juice and something else. I grabbed a small bottle of Dasani, and we walked past the waitrons toward Main Street, USA, where we could hear loud music coming from.

143

There, flanking both sides of Main Street, was the Florida A&M University marching band, serving as our welcoming committee. As the drums played and trumpets and trombones bellowed, we walked down Main Street with live music coming at us from both sides. It was a perfect early October evening. There was the band, the sky, and Cinderella's castle directly in front of us, off in the distance, magically changing from a soft pastel shade of blue to purple to pink. Unbelievable.

As we made it past the band and into the park, more food treats awaited us. Trays of cocktail shrimp the size of a large man's thumb. Crab claws and scallops. Oysters on the half shell. Petite racks of lamb, and an army of chefs in pastry hats, stir-frying, glazing, and presenting one culinary delight after another.

It was one big schmooze-fest by night, public relations bonanza by day. Rows of tripods and video cameras were stationed side by side at strategic locations throughout the parks. Disney's spinmasters had thought of everything. Brand-new umbrellas, still in their plastic wrappers, sat at the ready if inclement weather arrived. White tents were tucked discreetly behind live-shot locations and filled with portable air conditioners, bottled water, and makeup artists neatly arranging an array of elixirs and potions on tables, ready to transform tired and overheated journalists into TV stars.

Pat and I had gotten to our live location early, and I was able to watch the dance play out over and over; one talent after another lining up for live shots. The weather girl from Philadelphia, the entertainment reporter from Miami, all doing three- and four-minute hits for their local morning and noon shows. It was an assembly line of satellite shots. Fifteen minutes before you were "up on the bird" as they say, a crew of photographers, sound technicians, and lighting grips wearing sunscreen, T-shirts, and fishing hats would place you in position, plug in your earpiece, hand you a microphone, and check to see that everything looked as it should—water, tissue, powder. "Is my mike working?" A scramble on the audio board, and a thumbs-up. And then you were on.

"Hello, Twin Cities! It's a beautiful day here in Orlando...."

Once your live shot was over, you simply didn't matter anymore. Those same technicians who had just attended to your every need gave you a curt thank-you and good-bye-now-get-out-of-the-way-because-another-crew-is-coming. Because that's what the crew was paid to do: all day long, one right after another, make sure each and every talent got up on the bird and looked good.

Of course, I looked nothing like the other "talent," as they called us. They were weather girls in tight, jewel-toned, off-the-shoulder Lycra tops and even tighter-fitting white pants. They were from Miami and California, and exuded a type of on-air sex appeal in stark contrast to the professional image I was trying to project. Me, the girl from the Midwest in a station-issued polo shirt and khakis. Even at this stage in my television career, having made it to the fifteenth-largest television market in the country, which also happened to be my hometown, I still struggled with body issues. At times, I felt my on-air image didn't measure up. I was a brown girl in a white girl's world. A size 10 among size 0's. The Florida humidity turned my permed hair into fuzz, while the long blonde locks of my compatriots blew in the wind.

I stood there and watched as they flirted with the crew and oooed through their lip-gloss into the camera. I felt so inadequate, plagued with a plain-Jane image of myself that had haunted me since childhood.

Why is it so hard to embrace who we are? Maybe because we're barraged all day with messages that we aren't good enough, thin enough, pretty enough, rich enough. We live our entire lives thinking we just don't measure up and we never will. I'm right here with you sister, believe you me.

I spent much of my life thinking I was an ugly duckling.

From the time I was five, I wore glasses. My first pair were plastic light blue cat-eyes. The pair after that, oval black rims. I owned the nickname "Four Eyes." I was clumsy and wiry thin—"Toothpick" was another nickname. As was "Cakeface" when I started to learn how to wear makeup. The cruelty of playground taunts was the breeding ground for a lifetime of insecurities and low self-esteem.

I remember thinking, when I was about eleven or twelve years old, that if I could just be as beautiful as my mother, then people would love me the way they all seemed to love her. My beautiful brown-skinned, dark-haired, petite, and ultra-feminine mother. People often said she looked like the actress Diahann Carroll. I was so proud to have such a beautiful mother. She took a bath in Esté Lauder Youth Dew bubble bath, her favorite, every morning, and when she would open the door, the sweet rich smell of her bath oil would fill the upstairs hallway. She would powder and dress and comb her jet black hair into a soft ponytail and, without one stitch of makeup, become the essence of feminine beauty.

One morning, after her bath, I went into the bathroom and my child's imagination hoped, if not believed, that the lingering aroma would make me beautiful too. I wiped the steam away and peered into the bathroom mirror, and started to cry. Instead of the soft femininity that had greeted my mother's chocolate-brown reflection, I saw a lighter-skinned little girl with black, thick-rimmed glasses staring back. *I am not beautiful at all*, I thought.

Yet, God bless my mother.

She came back into the bathroom looking for a nail file and was startled to find me standing in front of the bathroom mirror crying. She asked me why my face was all tore up and I told her. I said, because I didn't look like her. Because I was ugly.

Without a word, my mother picked up a hairbrush and began to section off and brush my hair. I remember how lucky I felt to be getting her attention, which instantly made me start to feel better. She smoothed the edges down around my face and applied dabs of Ultra Sheen hair gel to make my hair shine. She reached into a drawer and pulled out a shiny red satin ribbon. She created a headband with the ribbon and tied a bow under my hair at the nape of my neck. When she finished, she turned my face to the mirror. The black-rimmed glasses were still there, but the unruly hair was now shiny and smooth.

"See there?" my mother said. "Fix your face, pretty girl."

147

Pretty girl. That's what she had called me. She located her nail file and left me standing in mirror reflecting on those two words.

Pretty girl. That was me. And yeah, for a moment, I did. I felt… pretty. From that day on "pretty girl" became my mother's moniker for me.

"Hey there, pretty girl," she would answer when I phoned.

"Hey there, pretty girl, it's Mom," she would say at the beginning of each voice mail. My mother taught me to own my authentic self, to stop comparing myself to what I might not ever be and embrace who I already was. My mother wore a 6 1/2 shoe. From the time I was in the sixth grade I wore a size 9 shoe. My mother was a petite size 6. I wore a 10. And it doesn't help that today's superstars are a size double zero. Right? But none of that matters. At some point and time we just have just have to say *enough*. This is who I am and I'm going to love me for me.

That's what I told myself that day in Orlando. Polo shirt and all. I'm good enough and in a few minutes I'd be up on the bird.

I know self-acceptance is tough, but it is also a paver on the path toward happiness. Being our authentic selves, however we get there, leads to joy.

Authenticity also extends far beyond physical appearance. In Panache Desai's book, *Discovering Your Soul Signature*, Desai, who was raised by a deeply spiritual family, takes the concept of authenticity even further by talking about authentic transparency. Beyond embracing how we look, true authenticity is the result of loving who we are. Desai writes:

> Authentic transparency is not about being transparent to other people. It is in fact, about being transparent to *yourself*. We've gotten to know our fear, sadness, anger, guilt, and shame. We've begun to take baby steps toward loving all these aspects of ourselves, just as the Divine loves us. Consider this: If we were honest with ourselves, how much easier would life become?[7]

Life would not only become way easier, but also more joyful. We'd spend time doing the things we really want to do, being with the people we really want to be with, saying what we really feel

148

The result of being our authentic selves, the result of being the real McCoy, is blissful, boundless, fearless, freedom and authentic joy.

Earlier I told the story of when I heard words, "You are free to be who God made you to be, and God will be with you," that gave me the courage to launch out into the deep and to be honest with myself by admitting that the time had come to leave my television career behind. That decision required a deep faith and trust that God would be there to see me through. Had I not trusted, had I not believed that God was with me, I believe this fantastical journey that I'm on as an author might not have ever occurred.

My faith gave me the courage to walk away from my broadcasting career and pursue my life-long dream of becoming a published author. My faith helped me to recognize and embrace my God-given gift of writing. This is something no one can ever take away from me because it is something I own internally. It has little to do with how I look or how much I weigh or what color my skin is or whether my hair is curly or straight. It just has to do with *me*.

149

I believe true joy in life comes when we can embrace who we are from the inside out. We're all good at something. Writing just happens to be my thing—what's yours? Discover it, embrace it, then run with it, because true joy comes from doing the things we're good at and the things we love.

Often, when I'm asked what makes me happy or how I define joy, my answer is simple: liking myself. Period. Liking who I am and who God made me to be. It goes far beyond cosmetics. Liking myself means being a person of integrity, a person of my word. It means being a good friend, someone somebody can rely on and trust. It means fervently pursing my passions. Telling the truth. Practicing kindness, giving thanks, and loving God. True freedom is true joy, and I believe we can only truly be free in life when we embrace who God made us to be. Whom the Son sets free is free indeed![8]

As a mentor once said to me, "You know, Roxane, I believe there are two kinds of people in life: people who are running scared and people who are running free." What I took away from that statement is this: freedom is truth.

Being authentic with ourselves is the first step to freedom. When looking for the joy in life, look to define who you are. What do you stand for? What are your gifts, talents and abilities? What are you good at doing? What means the most to you? Define the kind of work you would do for free just because you love it. Then start building a life that incorporates the answers to these questions. It'll take some doing, slowly, steadily, and intentionally. The path isn't always easy, but the reward for staying the course is joy.

150

10

SERVICE AND GENEROSITY

For God so loved the world that that He gave His only begotten son that whoever believes in Him shall not perish but have everlasting life.
—John 3:16

It is a commonly held belief that a life of service is a life of joy. At the very least, doing something for someone else gives us a sense of contribution. This was certainly true during the days and weeks following the 2016 presidential election. Politics aside, we can all agree it was one of the most divisive elections in recent history and left citizens feeling a need to *do something*. As a result, whether out of a sense of inspired altruism or anxiety-provoked despondency, charitable donations and volunteerism surged across the country.

Here in my hometowns of Minneapolis-St. Paul, more than one third of people already volunteer, making us the number-one big city in the country when it comes to volunteering.[9] Even with that, after the election, the number of calls to volunteer organizations increased dramatically across the Twin Cities. Big Brothers and Big Sisters, for example, saw inquiries about becoming a friend to a child in need triple. Community organizations that deliver meals or take in homeless teens reported an "unprecedented" increase in people wanting to help.

Why? Many people said the election motivated them to do more. Amid the anxiety people felt about the current political climate, people said it made them feel good and it gave them a sense of peace to do something for someone else. This speaks to the key to service— we do it because there is something about it we enjoy. In order to find joy and peace in giving, service to others must be something we *want* to do, not something we feel we *have* to do. No strings attached, no hidden agenda, no expectation of receiving something in return.

In his book *Happier*, Harvard professor Dr. Tal Ben-Shahar states that joy comes when there is a synthesis between what makes us happy and what brings happiness to others. He writes:

> Helping oneself and helping others are inextricably inter-twined: the more we help others, the happier we become, and the happier we become, the more inclined we are to help others.[10]

Dr. Ben-Shahar then includes this quote by Ralph Waldo Emerson: "It is one of the most beautiful compensations of life that no man can sincerely try to help another without helping himself." I have found this to be true in my own life. I found so much happiness in being a mom, reading story after bedtime story to my son when he was younger. Spending my days off taking him to the park and the zoo. Hearing his laughter and seeing his delight at what might otherwise seem mundane brought little sparks of joy and happiness into my life.

Our little home together brought us so much joy, often because we opened it up to others and shared what we had. It was music to my ears when we'd invite Jared's friends to sleep over and I'd hear them running up and down the stairs, giggling and laughing, playing hide-and-seek. One year I threw Jared a superhero sleepover birthday party. Every time the doorbell rang that night, a different superhero appeared. Batman. Spiderman. One kid wore a black suit and tie and came as one of the Men in Black.

Jared's dad had come over earlier to set up a video game system in the basement, in addition to the one we had upstairs in the living room, so there were kids running all over the house; in the basement, the living room, upstairs in Jared's room, in the kitchen for slices of pizza and soda pop. Sleeping bags were spread out on the living room floor and it must have been at least three in the morning before they all conked out. I ended up on the pullout sleeper sofa in the living room, after three exhausted superheroes had overtaken my bed and a couple more were knocked out in Jared's room.

In the morning I made waffles from scratch, fried bacon, scrambled eggs, and invited the boys to breakfast around our tiny dining room table. Some of their mothers came early to pick them up, and we all crammed around the table, eating waffles covered with bananas and strawberries and soaked in maple syrup.

The neighborhood, which was made up of clusters of single-family homes and detached townhomes, had a residents' pool, and in the summer my son's friends would come over and spend hours at the pool swimming. They'd run back to our house wrapped in damp

153

towels, stomachs rumbling from all the exercise. I'd make a small bonfire in our yard, and they'd roast hot dogs until the sun set.

I poured myself into being a mom because I loved it, and in many ways my career made me even more grateful for the time I was able to spend with my little boy. So much of my professional life involved covering other people's suffering. I saw more than my share of the not-so-pretty side of the human condition; accidents, crime, sickness, and death. Sometimes, in all honesty, it was hard to be objective and not feel some sense of empathy and loss for the names and faces that appeared on the evening news.

For example, each year in the spring, the station covered the Race for the Cure at the Mall of America. As part of the station's coverage, I was assigned to interview breast-cancer survivors. I will never forget one woman I interviewed. She was a mom with two daughters who had Stage 4 breast cancer. I interviewed her a couple of times over the years, and each time she wore a diamond necklace that her husband had given her. She explained to me that for each year she beat cancer, her husband added another diamond solitaire to the necklace. So far she had four perfectly round diamonds on a single silver chain. She told me she fully expected to fill the chain completely with diamonds.

After the interview I sat at their dining room table with her and her two young daughters as they made notecards to sell at the Race for the Cure. I was struck by the ease of their chatter and how normal and loving they appeared as they sat together, cutting paper and applying stickers and pink ribbon appliqués to folded pieces of cardstock. You never would have known anything was out of place or that this mother, with her quiet strength, was fighting for her very life. It would be the last time I saw her. She passed away from cancer a short time later. Two young daughters had lost their mom, and all I could do was post condolences on her CaringBridge page, go home, and hug my son.

Experiences like that made me even more grateful for my life and the small community of support I had found—kind and gracious neighbors who were there to help, the mothers of my son's classmates, who were more than willing to pick up my son from school when I got called out late on assignment. I had a faithful babysitter, named Tara, whom I could call at all hours on a moment's notice. She looked after my son like he was her own. And, of course, I had my parents, "Ger-pa" and "Ger-ma," as Jared called them, who were more than happy to babysit their grandson.

I had my own tiny little village in that tiny little townhouse in a tiny little neighborhood, and for the first time in a long time, I was happy. It was only years later that I learned the children I had invited into my home considered those summers at the pool, and sleepovers, and waffles, and bonfires among some of their favorite childhood memories. So we lived, mother and son, day in, day out, making memories out of everyday life.

Those sleepovers and waffle and bacon breakfasts at our tiny dining room table with Jared's friends and their moms produced lots and lots of laughter in our house. And so do a lot of little things, like bringing your husband or wife coffee just because, holding the door for a stranger, letting in the car in front of you, giving a panhandler five bucks, participating in a live auction at a charity fundraiser, volunteering with your neighborhood group, traveling with your church on a missions trip, bringing your aging parents bakery treats, helping your neighbor with a DIY project, volunteering at your kid's school, or volunteering anywhere for any amount of time for any cause you deem worthy. Some acts of service require resources and effort, but many don't; just your time, and maybe a little elbow grease, is all that's required. Giving and encouraging others to give is a timeless spiritual principle.[11] In helping others we help ourselves.

Take a moment to think about how you can make someone's day. Even when, especially when, your day might not be going so great. *"We must also consider how to encourage each other to show love and to do good things"* (Hebrews 10:24 GW).

The smallest act of service, kindness, and generosity can go a long way toward producing joy in your life. Think of it as a boomerang—what you give out will eventually find its way back to you. In other words, we reap what we sow,[12] so let's choose to give generously of ourselves and watch the blessings and joy enter our lives.

11

POSITIVE CONNECTIONS

Light shines on the godly, and joy on those whose hearts are right.
—Psalm 97:11 NLT

During a recent flight from Minneapolis to Los Angeles, I found myself seated next to *New York Times* best-selling author, journalist, and national talk show host Tavis Smiley. He was courteous and extremely engaging, and we talked about everything: books, television, film, travel, and his decades-long friendship with the late Maya Angelou. We must have chatted the entire flight. We talked a little politics, but not much. Which probably was a good thing. I was fascinated, instead, to hear about his career path as a national talk show host and author of several *New York Times* bestselling books. Whether or not I agreed with his opinions or prognostications, there's no denying that Tavis Smiley is a man in possession of a mind filled with ideas and opinions, which he didn't mind sharing. For nearly three hours, some thirty-five thousand feet in the air, our conversation percolated far above the clouds and far above the small talk and the gossip of the day. It was a conversation of great depth and substance. I listened intensely, saying very little, learning all that I could. His kindness and willingness to share his expertise on such topics as writing, film producing, and building friendships and lasting business relationships, created a positive connection between us as well as a great memory. It was a fantastical conversation, one I often think back on with a smile.

It's no secret that human beings are wired for such positive connections. We seek them out. And one secret I learned from my days as a television news reporter is that sometimes we can form connections without saying a single word. During my television career I was often recognized for my skills as an interviewer. Whether I was doing an in-depth sit-down interview with some famous person or out in the field getting a sound bite for a breaking news story, my managers would often remark at my ability to get people to open up and to access the heart of the story.

158

The secret was not so much in what I said, but in what I *didn't* say. The secret was that I listened. I would just let people talk and listen with the intent of really hearing what they were saying, rather than thinking about what I was going to say next. Listening in this focused way allowed me to formulate relative follow-up questions, delve deeper, and learn more, sometimes extracting little gems, pearls of wisdom and truth.

One Veteran's Day I was interviewing a war veteran being honored as a hero. I could tell by his body language that he wasn't comfortable talking about his service. When I asked him how he felt about being honored, he didn't offer much of a reply, deflecting my question. So finally I asked, "Do *you* think you're a hero?"

He looked down and shook his head no.

"Why not?"

He looked up at me and answered quietly, "Because I came back. The real heroes are my buddies, the ones who never made it back home."

With one sentence this veteran had shifted the focus from himself to honoring those to whom honor was truly due—his friends and fellow soldiers who had made the ultimate sacrifice. It was a poignant moment, one I'll never forget.

I've learned that listening and observing allows us to go deeper and form more meaningful and positive connections. Conversations have the power to connect, especially when we cut out the small talk and take the time to really listen.

159

But it also matters whom the conversations are *with*.

I think back to Jared's basketball games and track meets and the many hours and weekends sitting on wooden bleachers and metal chairs. I formed some great friendships during those years, including a wonderful friendship with one basketball mom named Kim. Her son Rick played basketball in the same league as Jared and often Kim and I would sit side by side chatting it up during games. Over time we began to talk about more than basketball. She loved anything that had to do with tea, from tea cups to tea parties, and so did I. She loved to cook and bake, and so did I. She loved God and so did I. When basketball season ended in the spring, Kim and I would go for long walks along the trails by her family's home. We would stop for coffee at a small coffee shop along the way and encourage each other in our faith walk. I invited her over for tea. And when our boys graduated from high school, I went to Rick's graduation party and visited with Kim's husband and members from Rick and Jared's basketball team. Before leaving the party, as Kim cried in my arms, I prayed with her for her son's safety and well-being. The next day Rick left to enter the Naval Academy.

My friendship with Kim was the kind of positive connection that breathed life into me. Kim helped me see the value in kindness and authentic friendship. She and her family helped me feel a little less lonely as a single parent. She encouraged me and I encouraged her.

The same can be said for my golf buddies, Deb and Kate. Unlike my friendship with Kim, I only saw Deb and Kate once a week on league nights during the summer. They were older than I and as we walked the course during those warm summer nights, they'd talk about their children and grandchildren. But what I remember most about Deb and Kate is that they never complained—about anything. They just seemed to have this joy about them. If either of them hit a bad shot, they'd say something like, "We'll get it right on the next hole." They were much better golfers than I and so I heard that a lot: "You'll get it right on the next hole, Roxane!" The times, for instance, when I'd hit a good shot off the tee, sending my ball long and straight down the fairway, I'd hear Kate's trademark phrase; "Now *that* was a thing 'a beauty!" I loved playing golf with those two ladies. They were funny, kind, and exuded a positive energy that was infectious. Our rounds of golf were filled with lots of laughter.

160

Of course it's a given that we all need to add more love and laughter to our lives. Joy is the by-product of becoming the kind of person others are happy to see and of surrounding ourselves with people who make us smile. Is there a Deb or Kate or Kim in your life? Someone who's willing to listen, who is positive and encouraging? Someone who makes you laugh? These are the kinds of connections that breathe life into all of us. Connections that go beyond the surface and help us feel heard, understood, supported, and even celebrated.

Meaningful and substantive conversations and memorable experiences with people we care about—our family and friends—produce joy. We feel heard. We learn something. We create a positive memory. We form connections, which is what all human beings are innately wired by God to do. Sometimes the best thing we can do for the people in our lives is to just listen. Positive, meaningful interactions draw us closer to one another and make us happy.

Throughout this book I've written about my effort to intentionally maintain a positive relationship with my ex-husband. This is something I chose to do. Something I did on purpose. I made a conscious decision to do what was needed to form an amicable co-parenting relationship with Keith for the sake of our son. That meant putting the past behind and moving forward. It meant allowing Keith to see his son whenever he wanted. It meant consciously working to include Keith in major decisions about Jared's life, from his healthcare to his college choices. For Keith it meant being supportive, responsible, and available. For the both of us, it meant focusing on the positive aspects of our relationship—the fact that we had a beautiful son whom we both deeply loved—and moving past the negative forces that had caused our marriage to end. I can tell you, it required putting on our big girl and big boy pants. It required maturity and selflessness. But our son grew up knowing he was loved by both of his parents. Whenever Jared saw his parents together, we were respectful and cordial toward each other. People would often ask me why Keith and I got divorced in the first place since we seemed to get along so well in public. All I can say is that remaining cordial took a great deal of effort, which reaped great reward. The effort we put into making the best of our situation helped us to live a life free from acrimony and discord. We chose to focus on our positive connection, our son, and that brought us joy.

I can't overstate the importance of positive connections in life.

162   That means the opposite is important, too. If someone is bringing you down, or is constantly negative, you might want to rethink your relationship with that person. You may have seen the meme that is going around the Internet that says: "You can never have a positive life with a negative person." I don't know who said that first, but it's true. Negativity sucks the very life out of us. If someone is always complaining, or gossiping, or always finding fault in something or worse yet is putting you down or highlighting your weaknesses while minimizing your strengths, that's the type of person you need to distance yourself from. Anyone who hurts you physically or emotionally should not be in your life. Period.

During the 2016 presidential election, there was a lot written and talked about in the media about narcissism: a personality disorder that causes a person to be abnormally self-absorbed. At the time, it was open for debate whether media reports that inferred a certain presidential candidate suffered from narcissism were based on conjecture or rooted in fact. Either way, the election brought public awareness about a personality disorder that until then I had known little about. Narcissists, named after the mythical Greek god Narcissus, lack empathy, cannot admit when they are wrong, and need an insatiable amount of attention and admiration. In short, they steal your joy. A narcissist is one of the most negative and damaging types of people to be around. A relationship with a narcissist should be avoided at all costs.

In her book *No More Narcissists!*, Dr. Candace V. Love says narcissists are hard to recognize because in the beginning of new relationships they appear to be loving and kind. Even charismatic. But that all soon changes:

163

> Because of the unfortunate psychology of narcissists, they are actually unable to love another person in a way that is deep, reciprocal, mutually respectful and satisfying. Narcissistic men are self-absorbed and can never really love or appreciate you. They only love and appreciate what you do for them—the way you look, your status, or your service to them. Focused solely on fulfilling their own needs, narcissistic men are unable to perceive things from another person's perspective or to relate to a partner with kindness, respect, and sensitivity.[13]

While Dr. Love refers to men, this type of person is incapable of forming a positive connection whether they are male or female.

The reason why people develop narcissistic traits and why people are attracted to narcissists is usually due to some type of trauma in childhood. Dr. Love says that narcissistic behavior at its worst is known as narcissistic personality disorder or NPD. A narcissist rarely, if ever, changes, and the only way to deal with a narcissist is to have no contact with them at all. Full no-contact. That's not to say everyone who exhibits negativity is a narcissist, but both negativity and narcissistic behavior are toxic, dysfunctional, and destructive. Look for positive connections in your life and avoid toxic relationships at all cost. Toxic people steal your time, your energy, and your joy.

Positive and negative connections exist both face-to-face and in the digital world. What types of people are you friending on Facebook or following on Instagram? What sorts of things are they posting? I am not ashamed to admit that I will unfriend people in a heartbeat if they post negative or mean-spirited comments. Ancient wisdom tells us to focus on things that are true, pure, noble, lovely, and good.[14] To that end, think about what you are feeding your brain, the types of articles you're reading, and websites you're looking at online. As a former news reporter, I believe it's important to stay informed and up-to-date on current events, but ironically, as someone who worked in the business, I'm also careful not to watch too much news, especially when the news cycle is filled with vitriol and people bickering at each other. On Twitter, I follow feeds that offer daily doses of encouragement and positivity, and I try to do the same with my tweets. I invite you to come on over for a dose of positivity![1]

---

1. You can follow me on Twitter @roxanebattle.

12

GRATITUDE

Give thanks to the God of heaven. His love endures forever.
—Psalm 136:26 NIV

One summer Saturday morning a few years ago, I got up early to go to the farmers' market, one of my absolute favorite things to do. I was looking forward to walking among the rows of flowers and fresh vegetables, drinking coffee, and doing business with the merchants. Yet on this particular morning, it was cloudy and overcast, and a steady light drizzle was falling. Who wants to go to the farmers' market in the rain? Half the fun was being outside in morning sun among crowds of shoppers hunting for bargains! I was tempted to go back to bed. *Perfect morning for sleeping in*, I rationalized.

Instead, I put on a hat, found my umbrella, and went anyway. The light rain had kept people away, so the market was far less crowded than usual. I walked among the rows and rows of flowers and neatly displayed vegetables, chatted with merchants, bought a few pots of petunias, and passed on the monster-sized sweet rolls slathered in thick cream cheese frosting, opting for fresh-squeezed orange juice instead. Here it was, seven-thirty in the morning, and the smell of roasted corn reminded me of why I love coming down to the market.

The food, flowers, and interesting people with their constant, quiet chatter. The white tents and long tables filled with silver jewelry, glazed clay pots, and tie-dyed shirts. It all made up the feel of a free, open-air street festival, even in the rain.

I was a little soggy by the time I headed back to the car, laden with flowerpots and a few jars of cinnamon-spiced honey. Because the market wasn't as busy, the merchants had cut their prices, so I bought batches of flowers for a song. As I drove home, the inside of my car smelled like fresh-cut peonies and grass. The rain began to let up, and I could tell the rest of the day would be beautiful, the way it always is when the sun comes out after the rain. That thought, combined with the thought of my peaceful morning at the market, was a nice little pocket of joy.

166

If happiness is dancing in the rain, joy is defying the rain.

There is so much to be grateful for, if we just pause for a moment and take a look at nature and the beautiful earth God created. It's all around us, in every season. Summer brings lush green grass, and placid glass-like lakes reflecting a powder-blue golden-lit sky. In the fall, the crisp air and bright sunlight creates glorious panoramic mosaics of golden yellows and bright crimson with the changing leaves. The winter brings frosted pine trees, glistening ice cycles, and pristine white snow made up of individual snowflakes that twinkle like jewels in the sunlight. And in the spring, soft gentle rain washes away the old and makes way for the new.

It's all around us, if we look for it. The sunrise or sunset over the ocean against a watercolor sky. The sleepy child with a bedhead stealing your pillow. The cool breeze coming through the screened window. Yes, even the cliché smells of fresh-cut grass and fresh-brewed coffee. Finding your keys. Holding hands. The warm breath and soft kiss of the love of your life. Taking your heels off. Crying it all out. The funny way toddlers misplace syllables and consonants. Food of any sort, so long as it's your favorite. A yard sprinkler and the neighbor's kids. Sleeping in. Getting up and out after too many dark days of not being able to. Reunions. Embraces. Winning. Healing. Hoping. Saying yes to "Are we there yet?" The sound of children singing when they think no one is listening. Eating when you're hungry. Warmth when you're cold. Compassion when your heart aches.

There's no denying life gets messy and hard. We, as human beings, are a flawed, fallible bunch. Sometimes we get it right; sometimes we don't. Yet if the very axis of human engagement hinges on the balance between heartache and happiness, which will you choose to see?

I challenge you—rather, invite you—to look for and find the joy just as I did that Saturday morning in the rain. Make the decision every day to find something, however small, to be grateful for.

Because gratitude is the precept for joy.

In Josie Robinson's book, *The Gratitude Jar*, she writes about how she overcame a life of sadness, alcoholism, and depression by being intentional about expressing gratitude for even the smallest things in her life. For thirty days, each night before bed, together with her four-year-old son, Lucas, Robinson would write down what they were each thankful for and put it in a jar. They were grateful for the simplest things; family, food, sunshine after a spate of gloomy days. Her son was grateful for a soft bed to sleep in at night, and a room full of toys to play in during the day.

From the moment I woke up until the time I sat in Lucas's bed each night, I was on the lookout for things to be thankful for, and it completely changed my perspective. Looking for good things all day was a lot different from concentrating on the stuff that annoyed me, which is what I used to do. No wonder I used to be so crabby—all I ever saw was the bad. I never stopped to notice any of the good, much less give thanks for it.

This new way of thinking, of noticing good things and being grateful for them, was causing me to *feel* different too. It was subtle, like turning up the volume a notch, but it was there.

I felt happier.[15]

Robinson goes on to describe a lunch date with one of her friends in which her friend commented how Robinson not only appeared happier, but actually "joyous" and "content." This is such a great example of how being intentional about finding those pockets of joy in life can enhance our life in so many ways.

I believe the more we give thanks the happier we feel. I look back and am so grateful for the people who helped me along my path in life, especially during my time in the wilderness. How grateful I was for other moms who would pick up my son from school when I had to work late covering a story, or the babysitter who would come at 3:00 a.m. when I had to go into work early. I was grateful for my parents, who showed unconditional love, supporting me through all my difficult decisions in life. When times got really hard, or when I felt really sad, I would look back and take note of the people in my life whom I knew were there for me, and they would give me hope. Hope that produced joy.

Back then, today and every day, what am I most grateful for? The presence of God. Throughout my life, my love for God continues to grow and has produced a peace that surpasses all understanding,[16] a joy that at times can't even be explained. It's just a knowing, a trusting, that everything will eventually work out. With faith, things have a way of working out for the good.[17] No, I don't believe that God makes bad things happen, but I do believe by choosing to believe for the better and trusting in a power greater and higher than myself, my faith sustains me. I've always believed better days are ahead. I guess that optimism I speak so much about is anchored in my faith.

169

During my days in the wilderness when I was a lonely and, at times, struggling divorced mom, I could have very easily chosen not to trust in something unseen.[18] Yet being raised in the church from the time I was born, I chose to believe, and to lead a spiritual life, and though at times I may have been tempted or felt forsaken, I've always managed to find my way back.

You love him even though you have never seen him. Though you do not see him now, you trust him; and you rejoice with a glorious inexpressible joy. (1 Peter 1:8 NLT)

In Max Lucado's book *You'll Get Through This: Hope and Help for Your Turbulent Times*, he writes:

> God surrounds us in the same way the Pacific surrounds an ocean floor pebble. He is everywhere—above, below, on all sides. We choose our response—rock or sponge? Resist or receive? Everything within you says harden the heart. *Run from God; resist God; blame God.* But be careful. Hard hearts never heal. Spongy ones do.[19]

In the time right after my divorce there were days when it was all I could do to get out of bed in the morning. I fought mightily to win the battle over loneliness and depression. There were mornings when I would drive to work and sit in the parking lot in my car and cry. I'd just cry and cry. I was tired and life seemed hard and my job was stressing me out, and so I'd cry. Then I'd wipe my face, get out of my car, walk into the television station and head straight for the dressing room where I'd put on a layer of under-eye concealer and makeup before heading out into the studio and on the air. I got good at masking my emotions, appearing to be happy and chipper in front of the camera, while deep down still feeling like a loser.

It didn't help that I suffered from seasonal affective disorder or SAD, a form of depression brought on by cloudy days in the winter. The lack of sunlight for days on end caused more than just the winter blues, it would send me into a deep, downward spiral emotionally. Taking large doses of Vitamin D seemed to help, but on really bad days, my mind would magnify all of my failures and flaws. I would struggle with the notion that divorce wasn't very

Christian-like. After all, the Bible states that God hates divorce.[20] Would God still love me? Would He still accept me? That's when I really had to come to grips with what I believed. I chose to believe what the Scriptures say, that God's love is unconditional, that neither height nor depth nor any living thing shall separate me from the love of Christ.[21] Yes, I'll have to answer for the divorce on judgment day. On that day it'll be between me and the Big Guy, and no one else.

But for now, I know I have felt the love of God in my life, through small miracles that seem to come out of nowhere. The raises and promotions that came during my television career, which helped me provide for my son, the kindness of my friends and family who were there from me when I needed them. I even consider my own mental sanity and stability a small miracle. Maintaining a presence of mind allowed me to continue to create and function effectively as a professional in a high-profile job as I worked to put my life back together.

171

Through it all, I never stopped thanking God for each new day, for another chance to try again and another chance to get it right. I thanked God for health and strength and my very life. I thanked God for love, mercy, and forgiving grace. His mercies are new every morning and my hope is in Him.[22]

Today, I still thank God every morning my feet hit the floor, for with each new day comes one more chance to look for and find life's joy.

13

SELF-CARE

Don't be dejected and sad,
for the joy of the LORD is your strength!
—Nehemiah 8:10 NLT

When is the last time you had a good cry? I mean a really good cry, where your eyes are red, your nose is running, your belly is shaking, and you just can't seem to stop? Been there, done that. A few months before Jared graduated from high school, I grabbed a box of Kleenex, my iPhone, and the mini Jambox Bluetooth speaker he had given me for Christmas (best Christmas present ever) and locked myself in the bathroom. I put one of my favorite worship songs on repeat and played it through the Jambox. Praise music filled the bathroom and bounced off the walls. I grabbed the tissue box, sat on the edge of the bathtub, and just bawled.

In a few short months, Jared was going to be heading off to college and every time I thought about becoming an empty nester, my eyes would tear up but I'd stuff my emotions down. When Jared brought home the order form for his graduation cap and gown, I stuffed it. When I went to get groceries and saw the graduation cakes in the bakery case, I'd stuff it. Every time a grad party invite from one of his friends came in the mail and the whole time I planned his graduation party, I stuffed it. Finally, I decided enough stuffing. There, while locked in the bathroom, plowing through tissues, I let it all out. I had a really good cry. I don't know how long I was in there, maybe an hour or so, but eventually I was all cried out. I had stopped stuffing and accepted the fact that my baby was leaving home.

And you know what? After that cry, I felt better. That's not to say I still wouldn't be sad and cry when the actual day came, but allowing myself to work through my emotions helped me accept and cope with this new season in my life.

And science bears me out. A Minnesota biochemist by the name of Dr. William Frey wrote a book called *Crying: The Mystery of Tears*. Dr. Frey discovered that a good emotional cry actually releases stress hormones from our bodies, making us feel relaxed.[23] It also makes us feel better because it produces endorphins, or "feel good" hormones. It truly feels good to cry. It's a healthy exercise and an important part of taking care of ourselves.

In an episode of *Downton Abbey*, the matriarch Violet Crawley, Dowager Countess of Grantham, says in one of her trademark rejoinders that "a lack of compassion can be as vulgar as an excess of tears." That's a witty summation of the antiquated belief that crying is socially unacceptable, or a sign of weakness. I disagree. I think crying is actually a sign of strength because it demonstrates the courage to honor and work through our emotions. It's healthy to release all those stress hormones instead of stuffing them. Do I dare postulate that allowing ourselves to feel sad can eventually make us feel, well, happy? That may be a stretch, but it's also biblical truth: *"Weeping may endure for a night, but joy comes in the morning"* (Psalm 30:5). Allowing yourself to feel what you feel in a safe and supportive environment is an important part of taking care of yourself.

So is sleep. Couldn't we all use more of it? And yet the demands of life make it so hard to get in a good eight hours! A good night's rest may be more important to our overall health and well-being than we realize. Studies show that increasing the amount of sleep working moms got by just one extra hour per night led to increases in their income and job satisfaction.[24] Sleep scientists can even predict which games NBA teams will lose based on their sleep schedules.[25] Knowing that professional athletes routinely crisscross the country en route to game venues on lengthy overnight flights, sometimes arriving in the wee hours of the morning, scientists looked at the amount of rest star players got and compared that to their performance on the court. Not surprisingly, they concluded athletes play better and get injured far less when they get more rest.

In one of the last games in the 2016–2017 NBA regular season, the Minnesota Timberwolves beat the number-one ranked Golden State Warriors 103–102 in a playoff-like atmosphere at home in the Target Center, before a record capacity crowd of twenty thousand fans. The Warriors were playing without injured star Kevin Durant, yet the game featured quick, energetic play, especially from the Warrior's superstar Stephen Curry, who tied the game with a shot late in the fourth quarter. With less than thirteen seconds to go, Timberwolves star Andrew Wiggins, who had missed two free throws just seconds earlier, was fouled and stepped to the line, winning the game with two free throws—one to tie, the other for the win. It was the Warrior's fourth loss in eleven days, which sportswriters described as a "cataclysmic slump" for the superstar team.[26] Post-game, the Warriors groused to reporters, blaming bad officiating for the loss, while head coach Steve Kerr, on the other hand, told reporters that he would be resting Curry and three other top players the next night in San Antonio.

It was as controversial decision; resting marquee players before a big game, much to the disappointment of San Antonio fans who bought tickets thinking they would be seeing the superstars in action. The Warriors lost to San Antonio 85–107. Meanwhile the Minnesota Timberwolves, who had been on a late-season winning surge, traveled to Milwaukee the day after beating the Warriors and lost to the Bucks 95–102. After three straight days of rest, the Warriors returned home to play the thirteenth-ranked Philadelphia 76ers. In the fourth quarter, the 76ers blew a 12 point-lead and the Warriors won 106–104.

In the NFL, teams get one week off during the season to rest, which is called a bye week. Racecar drivers stop to refuel. Rest during the course of our lives is so important. The biggest obstacle to obtaining it, aside from bouts of insomnia and the fact that we're all getting less of it, is the perception that sleep is wasted time; we believe that we're being lazy or unproductive when we sleep.

The reality is just the opposite. The body heals and the mind restores when we sleep. Proper rest helps maintain good health and keeps weight gain at bay. (We eat more when we're tired.) The fountain of youth is found on our pillow. The better rested we are, the more clearly we can think and the more productive we can be. We may think we're doing nothing by lying unconscious for seven to eight hours, but the brain is actually quite busy flushing out the toxins of the day, much like the dishwashing machine in your kitchen scours over pots and pans, methodically rinsing away the debris from last night's dinner plates.[27] That may explain why we dream what we dream, as our minds replay the day's thoughts. In the morning after a good night's rest, the body and mind are refreshed—ready to reason, think, and problem-solve.

Right after I left my television news career, I would take long naps in the afternoon. It was some of the most restful sleep I had experienced in years. I believe those naps, during a time of intense transition, helped me approach the task of moving on with my life with a clearer head.

Like many of you, there are many times when my mind is racing so fast I can't fall asleep, but I have found a few things that help. I keep the bedroom temperature cool and I don't have any electronics in my bedroom, not even a television. A cool, dark environment free from blinking lights and electronics gives me the best shot at a good, uninterrupted night's rest. I'm super sensitive to smells so I have also found spritzing my pillow with or inhaling eucalyptus or lavender scented oil helps me fall off to sleep.

But resting during the night isn't the only rest that's needed. During the day, I encourage you to take a time out every now and then. Take a few moments to meditate or pray, pause for a few moments, collect your thoughts, and catch your breath. Get in a quick twenty-minute catnap if you need it. Rest, even in its smallest increments, is a huge part of taking care of ourselves.

Things often got really hectic at the television station, with producers and reporters all scrambling under deadline pressure to make the evening news. In the midst of all of that, I would go into the ladies' room, turn on the warm water, squirt some soap from the dispenser into my hands, and slowly and very methodically wash my hands. I'd work up a good lather, feeling the soap between my fingers, and after a few moments slowly rinse the lather away, letting the water warm my hands. I'd then, while looking in the mirror, dry my hands, take a deep breath, and go back to work.

I know that may sound weird, but something as simple as taking a break from the newsroom to go wash my hands was a small but effective de-stressor. I learned that taking short breaks during the day is just as important as getting rest at night. Now, I start every morning in quiet contemplation, giving thanks for the new day ahead. *"You will give me back my life and give me wonderful joy in your presence"* (Acts 2:28 TLB).

When my son was young and needed my constant care, I would use the time he spent with his father to sleep and to exercise, another big part of taking care of myself. Good health is everything. I had a routine of going down to the health club around suppertime on Saturday evenings. The club's large swimming pool was often empty at that time, and I would dive in the water and swim laps up and down the pool. I'd do the backstroke and look up at the florescent lights in the ceiling, and as I felt and heard

177

the water splashing about me, I'd think about the week—what went wrong, what went right. I'd think about the feature report I was working on at the time and craft sentences in my head that would later find their way into scripts, which would eventually air on TV. And sometimes I wouldn't think at all; I'd just listen to the water and my own breathing as I swam. Afterwards, I'd head to the sauna and let the smell of eucalyptus fill my nostrils, getting lost in thought as I sat engulfed in steam. After my workout, I'd shower and dress, grab a cold glass of water from the dispenser in the lobby, and head home. This was my time and it helped me cope. The swim helped me stay in shape and the time alone helped me clear my head. During those dark, quiet drives home from the health club, I often felt at peace.

Eventually I started jogging. Just like my son, I had run track in high school and even competed at the state level, but it had been years, even decades, since I had laced up a pair of running shoes. The day I ran a full mile, I felt such a sense of accomplishment that I decided to work up to running two, and then three miles. Picking up running again when you're middle-aged is much different from running in high school, but I took it slow and kept going, gradually increasing my running distance over time. I was well into my forties by the time I competed in the Iron Girl, a 26-mile duathlon, running two miles, biking twenty-two miles, and running another two miles. I had trained for months during the summer, going on fifteen-mile bike rides by myself, and jogging mile after mile up and down the street where I lived.

That fall, when I completed the 26-mile race course, something inside of me changed, permanently. As I crossed the finish line, a volunteer handed me a bottle of water and put a medal dangling from a pink grosgrain ribbon around my neck that said "Finisher." As another volunteer bent down and removed the timing chip strapped around my ankle, I looked around and saw other finishers cheering and laughing as their family and friends congratulated them on finishing the race. I stood there in this celebratory atmosphere with loud music blaring from the outdoor speakers and pink banners waving in the wind. I looked deeper into the crowd and that's when I saw other women crying and hugging. Pink grosgrain ribbons and medals hanging from their necks, their arms wrapped around each other. Some of them had run this race after losing weight and vowing to get physically fit. And they had done it. Some of them had run this race in the memory of a sister, mother, or best friend who had died from breast cancer. And they had done it. They had honored themselves and their loved ones with their sheer might, willpower, and strength.

Let me tell you, when you're standing on the other side of the finish line, hot, sweaty, and out of breath, after running and biking for the better part of two hours, knowing that all you had to give was your all, it's pretty powerful stuff. An experience like that, if you let it, has the power to touch your soul, to tap into the very essence of your humanness, and leave you forever changed.

I had a new, heightened sense of self-esteem. I had taken on a huge challenge, and even though I was one of the last racers in, I had finished. I kept looking in disbelief at the finisher's medal they had placed around my neck. I couldn't believe I had done it, and now I was hooked; I wanted to earn more hardware. I did the Iron Girl race four years in a row, each time getting better and faster and improving my finishing time. Jared was at every single race, cheering me on from the crowd. I always teared up when they sang the National Anthem at the start. It made me feel like a bona fide athlete. I loved everything about the race environment: the banners waving in the wind, the DJ playing music over loudspeakers to pump up the runners, and the crowds of family and friends who lined the course, shaking cowbells and waving banners to cheer us on.

My point in all of that is that exercise is my way of taking care of myself and striving toward being the best version of me. Admittedly, there are times when I have a love-hate relationship with running, but once I get in shape, I enjoy it a great deal. Running 5Ks and competing in marathons and bike races isn't for everyone, I get that. Yet it is important that we all see ourselves as important enough to be worth taking care of. Getting enough rest, exercising, and eating healthy foods are all vital to self-care.

Be good to yourself in whatever healthy and positive way helps you find joy. When life gets crazy, find a way to take a few moments and restore yourself. Take time for you, even if it's just for five minutes. Close your eyes and breathe deeply.

Adding beauty to your environment also adds joy. The next time you're at the grocery store, buy yourself a bouquet of flowers, just because. Why wait to have company over to break out the special dishes? And yes, if that new pair of shoes or hot fudge molten chocolate cake makes you happy, go for it, all in moderation. Just remember to take care of and be good to *you*.

Here's why; because you matter. Don't listen to anyone who tells you that you don't, especially yourself. Stop the negative self-talk. You are an amazing creature made in the image of God.[28] And as I'm sure you've heard it said, "God don't make no junk." Be kind to yourself and allow yourself to dream, because your dreams matter. Your ideas matter. You, as a living, breathing human being, matter. You are a person of substance, worthy of consideration, capable of making a difference in this world, however great or small, because you matter, which is all the reason you will ever need to remember to take care of YOU.

14

YIELDING

Think of the various tests you encounter as occasions for joy.
After all, you know that the testing of
your faith produces endurance.
—James 1:2–3 CEB

This one takes a little visualization, and a big dose of humility. Just stay with me here.

Picture in your head that you're just about to merge onto a busy road and you see in the median a big red-and-white "yield" sign. The purpose of the yield traffic sign is to alert oncoming drivers to slow down and allow others to pass. A yield sign gives other drivers the right of way. I think this is a great metaphor for human relationships, because yielding speaks to the art of compromise.

Years ago, my dear friend Karen had her mother-in-law Ruth come live with her, and right from the start, things didn't go well. Karen was used to running her household one way, and Ruth was use to running things another way. Even though it was Karen's house, Ruth wanted the right of way, and almost daily the two of them were at odds over little things, like what to cook for dinner or whether to wash the dishes by hand or put them in the dishwasher. Karen liked Skippy peanut butter, but her mother-in-law would buy Jif. Karen liked Miracle Whip mayonnaise; her mother-in-law bought Hellman's. Despite having an ample supply of bargain laundry detergent on hand, Ruth went out and bought a box of Tide.

Karen was incensed. She always used the bargain detergent; it was what her family was used to, and she viewed the box of Tide and the jars of Jif and Hellman's as duplicitous and unnecessary expenses and she said so. Yet Ruth was unmoved and continued to use Tide to do the laundry (while munching on a Jif peanut butter sandwich or tuna on rye with Hellman's).

Then there was Ruth's habit of letting raw meat thaw out on the kitchen counter. This sent Karen through the roof as she thought about the germs and diseases her husband and children could contract as a result. Yet despite Karen's pleas, Ruth continued what Karen saw as a disgusting habit.

183

It wasn't long before Karen started to feel stressed out as the smallest disagreements grew into major flare-ups. Karen would leave the house each morning fuming, grumbling under her breath about why her mother-in-law was so set in her ways. After all, Karen thought, this was her house and Ruth was essentially a guest.

Karen told me how she walked out one morning in a rage, thinking as she drove to work, *Why is my mother-in-law so rigid? Why does she always have to get her way? Why does she always have to be right?* Then, something amazing happened. There, alone in her car, while driving into work, she had an epiphany: *Wait a minute*, Karen thought. *Why am I so rigid? Why do I always have to get my way? Why do I always have to be right?* After all Ruth had raised Karen's husband and his four siblings and they had all lived to adulthood and none of them had contracted dysentery or Ebola or any sort of horrible foodborne disease. Is peanut butter and mayo really that big of a deal? And what does it matter what type of laundry detergent we use as long as everybody in the house has clean socks and underwear?

That day after work, Karen stopped by the grocery story and bought a box of Tide, a jar of Jif peanut butter, and a jar Hellman's mayonnaise. When she got home, she sat the grocery bag on the kitchen counter and said to Ruth, "Here you go, Mom, I'd thought you'd enjoy these."

184

Because Karen yielded and admitted to herself that, just possibly, *she* was the rigid one, she and her mother-in-law were able to coexist peacefully under the same roof until the day came when Ruth left this earth.

Arguments and disagreements are stressful and make us feel miserable. Yet, being a little bit more willing to do our part to smooth over conflict, and yes, sometimes compromise, especially with the small stuff, can help us live a more stress-free and joy-filled life.

It takes courage and humility to yield. Sometimes I really think that when we resist, we don't acquiesce because we're afraid it will make us appear weak, when in reality considering the needs of others above our own is actually a sign of strength. I'm not advocating becoming a doormat or allowing ourselves to be taken advantage of, I'm simply saying that when it comes to the small, inconsequential things in life like food choices or who gets to pick the movie on movie night, yielding can produce joy.

So much of our existence on this planet is defined by our human relationships and how we engage, connect, and get along with others. In Timothy Keller's book, *The Meaning of Marriage*, he explains that humility can go a long way toward resolving conflicts in marriage, and I think this can also be applied to most of our relationships:

> One of the most basic skills in marriage is the ability to tell the straight unvarnished truth about what your spouse has done—and then, completely, unself-righteously, and joyously express forgiveness, without a shred of superiority, without making the other person feel small.[29]

185

I know what you're thinking; easier said than done. You're right. Perhaps because we all harbor insecurities about being taken advantage of or being wrong. This is where we must trust our friends, our family, and our own instincts that tell us it's okay to allow ourselves a certain degree of vulnerability in our relationships. Sometimes that vulnerability means yielding for the greater good.

Being able to successfully manage conflict through the art of compromise goes a long way toward living a life of peace and joy. In order to do this, Keller points toward exercising humility, but also having a certain confidence and joy about yourself. If you feel good about yourself, you'll be more willing to consider the feelings of others and have an easier time navigating conflict. We talked about the importance of self-care in the previous chapter.

Ironically, taking care of yourself also gives you the courage and confidence to not make everything all about you all the time. A healthy dose of self-esteem doesn't leave us wanting and allows us to exercise, when needed, a little appropriately-timed diplomacy and consideration.

I remember my divorce attorney telling me to never disparage or bad-mouth my ex-husband in front of our son. Even though we had our adult differences, it was important for Jared's growth and development that we not speak poorly about each other because he loved both of his parents. All while Jared was growing up, Keith and I worked to maintain cordial and respectful communication between the two of us. At basketball games, during pick-ups and drop-offs, and any time we were with our son, we kept it positive. This required both of us to do a lot of yielding. We had to let go of the past, and focus on what was best for our son.

Earlier I wrote about how I passed up a career opportunity out of state so that my son could grow up near his dad. That was not an easy decision, but the joy that resulted made it all worth it. Jared's childhood is filled with memories of his father coaching his football and basketball teams, and father-and-son road trips during summer break or Saturday afternoon trips to the zoo. Looking back I have no regrets about the decision I made to turn that job down. At that moment in my life, it wasn't about me. It was about a boy and his dad, and my decision to pass a career opportunity was my way of yielding—trying to make the best of a not-so-good situation.

As the years went by, Jared and his father maintained their bond, and his father and I put our differences aside and became friends. Keith was there in the stands the day our son became a state track and field champion. He showed up an hour early for our son's high school graduation and he was there the day we sent our son off to college. Keith and I were both grateful that Jared had chosen to attend a state college just an hour and half out of the Twin Cities. It would be easy for him to come home some weekends if he wanted. Yet the reality was he would no longer be living with me or his dad.

It was a blistering hot Friday afternoon in August, and we had spent all day moving Jared into a dorm room that seemed no bigger than one of those movable storage containers. We had hauled up his futon and unpacked his sneakers and sweatshirts. Keith had made numerous trips to the electronics store to buy cords and cables for Jared's computer and TV. By the end the day, we were hot, sweaty, and tired. Jared was all moved in and now it was time for his mother and father to go home for the first time without their son. Even though we lived in separate nests, as of that day, both Keith and I were officially empty nesters.

It's something to see a grown man fighting back tears.

Keith struggled to maintain his composure as the three of us rode down the elevator together, in silence before we said good-bye. "I've been dreading this day," he had told me. And here it was. When the elevator stopped down at the lobby, the three of us got off and walked out into the parking lot in silence. I watched as Keith hugged his son goodbye and told him to call if he needed anything. "Love you, Dad. Thanks for everything," Jared told his father. Keith then, doing his best to feign a smile, glanced over at me, waved goodbye, got in his car, and drove away.

Jared and I then walked over to the bookstore to buy the last of the books he would need when classes started that Monday. The two of us then headed to my car. Out of habit, Jared opened the passenger door and slung his book bag on the floor and then quickly realized he wasn't coming with me. For the first time in his life, we were going separate ways. "Oh yeah, that's right," he said to himself as he took the books back out of the car and closed the door. I hugged him and told him I loved him and was proud of him and that I'd be back for Parents' Weekend. "Love you, Mom. Thanks for everything," he said.

188

As I drove off campus I looked in the rearview mirror to see one last glimpse of my son as he ran back to his dorm. On the way back to the cities I fought the lump in my throat as a few warm tears welled up and escaped down my cheeks spilling with little plops onto my shoulder. But that was it. I thought I would be a hot mess but I couldn't cry. I thought back on the day and how Keith and I had worked side by side just like we had all these years and I realized this is what we had been working toward. This is what all those parent-teacher conferences and curriculum nights were all about. The cartons of Crayolas and mechanical pencils. Book nook and parent nights. The piles of registration forms and fees. Campus tours and college entrance exams. Church camp and Sunday school. And yielding.

All of that was for this day; the day we sent our adult son out into the world on his own.

When I got back to the cities, I called Keith and told him he had done a good job with our son. His voice was shaky; I could tell he was still emotional. He thanked me for calling and told me he thought we had a great kid. I agreed.

Later that night, I went on Jared's Twitter feed and saw he had tweeted this: "All moved in. Man, I have the best parents in the whole world."

Yielding, I believe, had paid off.

A few years later, when I wrote this book, I asked my ex-husband to yield again because I needed his blessing. I had no idea how Keith was going to respond to a book about our divorce, about our son, and about co-parenting.

189

So I called him and asked. We made small talk for a few minutes, talking about our son and how he was doing, and then I told him I had written a book about the years that followed our divorce. At first he was silent on the other end of the phone, but what he said next absolutely floored me.

"I always thought you should write about those years," he said.

"Excuse me?" I asked.

"Yeah," he said, "I always thought you should write about those years. I think that's great."

We talked some more, and I then e-mailed him a few chapters so he could see what I had said about him. With his permission, here is the response he e-mailed me back:

You used the words "exemplary father," but I would say I simply tried to do what was needed and required as a father to support my son and his overall well-being during some extremely difficult days. During that time, I saw many men in similar situations shrink away, stating the situation was unfair and emasculating, without dignity or without any real way to prevail and win. Yet I chose to endeavor to do my best as a father, regardless of the obstacles, circumstances, or even the indignity of it all. Through the grace of God, I somehow understood winning as a father to be a different long-term equation and outcome than many other fathers in similar situations.

190

Thank you for the acknowledgment. In the end, after the child is raised, that acknowledgment is all that a father could ever want or ever hope to receive from the mother of his child.

15

FORGIVENESS

Forgive as the Lord forgave you.
—Colossians 3:13 NIV

Oh yeah, forgiveness is a biggie. That's why I saved it for last.

Let's unpack this slowly. Let's first look at why, if we are ever going to be happy, forgiveness is absolutely necessary. Then let's talk about whom we all need to forgive, and finally, I'd like to share why I forgave my ex-husband.

In Marianne Williamson's book, *Tears to Triumph: The Spiritual Journey from Suffering to Enlightenment*, she says forgiveness is the most essential key to happiness:

Forgiveness is a process and it doesn't mean the person we forgive will necessarily be our friend—for a while, or ever. If you've done something awful to me or to someone I love, I don't see myself hanging out with and having lunch with you anytime soon. If a woman lives with an abuser, she needs to leave the relationship. Forgiveness does not mean there are no boundaries, accountability, laws, or healthy standards of behavior. It means merely that there's a way for us to find peace in our hearts, regardless of someone else's behavior.[30]

Williamson says oftentimes our ego gets in the way of forgiveness and, while forgiveness is a process that's not always easy, it is a process that always comes with reward. And I would say part of that reward is emotional freedom and joy, especially when it comes to forgiving ourselves.

> *Those who look to Him for help will be radiant with joy; no shadow of shame will darken their faces.* (Psalms 34:5 NLT)

It's time to let go of the demons that dog our tracks, and gnaw away at our self-esteem. So you think you're the only one with a secret? Guess again. If walls could talk they would be drowned out by the sound of rattling bones. You've heard the quote, by Alexander Pope, "to err is human, to forgive is divine." We've all made and will continue to make mistakes, we've all done things we wish we hadn't. But what good comes from replaying past failings? Learning from our mistakes is one thing, but playing an endless loop of regret over and over in our heads and beating ourselves up over what we've done is another, so let it go—you've suffered enough. Make your mistakes, then make your mistakes matter, by learning from them and moving on.

My faith has shown me that God doesn't remember our failings; He has separated our good from our bad as far as the east is from the west.[31] If you think about it, the east and the west go in different directions and never meet. Whatever you've done that you feel bad about, whatever you've done that has left you burdened with a heavy secret, whatever it is that terrifies you at the thought of other people finding it out, whatever it is that has you feeling ashamed, if you are truly sorry and have repented and made amends, then it's over.

The word "repent" simply means to choose, to decide to change your mind, and not to repeat the same bad behavior. To truly live a life of joy, we must learn to let go of the past. It's over. You can let it go. Just because you made a mistake does not mean you *are* a mistake. Free yourself from the darkness and hidden pits of yesterday and head toward the light. Instead of what was, imagine all that can be. Start focusing on what's in front of you today as you imagine a better tomorrow. When you open yourself up to self-forgiveness, you end your own personal suffering, and begin to create the possibility of joy.

Grant me the ultimate joy of being forgiven!
(Psalm 51:8 NET)

193

Once we learn to forgive ourselves, it will be easier to forgive others. My dear friend and fellow author Deborah Smith Pegues wrote a beautiful book, *Forgive, Let Go, and Live*. I love this book for its candor and honesty, and also because of the beautiful light blue butterfly that is featured on the cover. We all know about how I feel about butterflies. Anyway, Deborah took the time to collect stories from everyday people about their real-life struggles with forgiveness. The book is filled with stories of forgiveness for all sorts of situations including infidelity, sexual abuse, domestic violence, and even murder. Heavy stuff.

There is one story in the book that really stood out to me. It was the story of a woman whose husband had been killed as a result of a drunk driver. He was riding home on his motorcycle when a car pulled out in front of him. Her husband had no time to stop, crashed into the car, and died instantly. The driver and the passenger of the car got out and ran. They eluded police for a several days before they were finally caught and jailed. They were both undocumented workers who eventually escaped from jail and were never seen again or brought to trial. This miscarriage of justice only added to the wife's deep grief over losing her husband, and for a long time she harbored hate for the man and anger at God.

She was a Christian woman who took solace by working at her church's food pantry. One day she got an e-mail stating that a family of five needed food. She looked at the address in the e-mail and thought God was playing a cruel joke on her. The address was the home of the family of her husband's killer. How could this be? She thought about deleting the e-mail. Yet, even though she was angry with God, her compassion for the woman and her four children won out.

Deborah Smith Pegues quotes the woman as she tells what happened next:

> With my face to the floor and my tears flowing, I forgave this man. I pleaded with the Lord to forgive me for all the hatred and resentment I had been carrying around for so long.
>
> The next weekend, I carried the box of food up the tiny steps to their trailer. I met the mother and her four beautiful children. It was bittersweet but truly a blessing. I did not mention that we had a common connection. She will never know how it came to be that the wife of the man her husband killed was sitting in her

living room with a box of food. She will never know how much I wanted to tell her, but instead prayed with her and over her family. My heart was bursting, and it took all I had not to break down in her home that day. God gave me the strength to face her and to love her as though she were my neighbor. It didn't matter that day that she was Hispanic or poor. It did not matter that she couldn't speak English or that I couldn't speak Spanish. All that mattered was that God has forgiven me and I had forgiven her husband. In that moment, I felt great joy.[32]

My goodness, every time I read that story, my eyes fill with tears. What it must have taken for that wife to forgive her husband's killer and extend compassion toward his family! In the end, her forgiveness brought great reward. Her forgiveness brought healing. Her forgiveness brought freedom. Her forgiveness brought joy.

195

In the widely read and often quoted book *The Return of the Prodigal Son: A Story of Homecoming*, its author, Henri J. M. Nouwen, writes about the power of reconciliation and forgiveness. Nouwen states that forgiveness:

> demands of me that I step over the wounded part of my heart that feels hurt and wronged and that wants to stay in control and put a few conditions between me and the one whom I am asked to forgive. This "stepping over" is the authentic discipline of forgiveness.[33]

And so then, in my desire to live a peaceful and happy life, I knew I too had to step over whatever hurt I felt as a result of the irreconcilable differences that led to my divorce. I had to forgive myself and forgive my ex-husband over a marriage that had failed. As I stated earlier on, the reasons are private, but the result of our mutual forgiveness is something to be shared.

In the previous pages of this book, you read about how we intentionally worked on an amicable co-parenting relationship. I could set my watch to the regularity in which my child support payments arrived. My ex never missed a payment. I allowed him to see his son whenever it worked, and we both behaved as cordial adults in the presence of our son. No name-calling. No bickering. No blaming.

And you know what? It worked. We put the past behind us, and as broken as we were, when the three of us were all together at the same time, whether at a game, or after a band concert, or over spaghetti at Keith's favorite Italian restaurant, my tiny family came together in the name of peace.

196

Now that our son is an adult, I look back on my life as a working divorced mom, and I have many positive memories of how we successfully navigated a functional co-parenting relationship. I decided it was time to write about it, with the hope that our journey would inspire others, maybe even you, to do the same.

As Henri Nouwen has shown us, to truly, authentically forgive someone, we must step over our desire to avenge whatever wrong we may have suffered. True forgiveness means we must step over our fear of being hurt again. True forgiveness requires that we not act out of vengeance, but rather we must act out of compassion, because only then will true forgiveness lead us to a place of joy, peace, and divine love.

EPILOGUE

Jared graduated from college on a beautiful Saturday morning the first week in May, and all I can say about that day is it was absolutely perfect—full of harmony, peace, deep, contented joy, and love, all marking a ceremonial end to our parenting journey.

There were three commencement ceremonies on campus that day with Jared's college, Arts and Humanities, graduating first at 9 a.m. The day before, I had spoken at a day-long women's conference and gotten home at 6:30 in the evening. I quickly packed an overnight bag with a few essentials, grabbed the silk and linen dress I had ordered online just for the graduation ceremony, and hit the road. I had chosen to drive down to the campus the night before and get a good night's rest before the ceremony rather than leaving at the crack of dawn and risk getting stuck in traffic. I pulled into town just after 9 p.m., checked in the hotel, and called my son. We were both hungry but most of the restaurants in town were closing so Jared said he'd order a pizza for the both of us and head right over. He arrived about forty minutes later, and there we sat, in a ground floor hotel room with the lights from the parking lot shining in through the window, listening to the occasional low rumble of semi-trailers barreling down the highway. This was the same hotel I had stayed in when I came for freshman orientation and Parents' Weekend. The same hotel I had stayed in the night before the few Division II track meets Jared ran in, until academics won out over collegiate sport and he stopped competing all together. Here we were again, one last time, sitting around a pizza box spread out on the hotel room desk, sharing a pepperoni pie and sipping on complimentary bottles of room temperature water. He had just finished finals week, I had been at a conference all day and we were both exhausted, yet so very much looking forward to tomorrow morning.

"I'm happy," Jared said quietly.

"Me too, Son."

We finished the pizza and, as Jared got ready to leave, I hugged his neck and began humming an obnoxious off-key version of Pomp and Circumstance in his ear, which made him giggle.

"Quit it, Mom."

He looked down at the floor and smiled a gentle smile that made my eyes mist. His father would be arriving in the morning and we made plans to meet up with him on campus at 7:30 a.m. With that, my son left for his apartment and I headed to bed.

The next morning, I drove to campus and found a parking spot right across the street from the arena where the ceremony would be held. The campus was so quiet and peaceful at 7:30 in the morning. The peace I felt pulling into campus was a precursor to how I would feel the entire day. It was as if God had provided angels as tour guides on one of the most important days of my life. Everything was going to be perfect.

198

I walked to the field house where the graduates were just starting to line up and waited in the hallway for Jared to arrive. The minute I saw him, I started to cry—tears of joy. He was dressed in a shirt and tie, carrying his cap and tassel and wearing his graduation gown. I hugged him and cried even harder.

"C'mon now Mom, I haven't even graduated yet," he said.

"Sorry, Son, sorry, I can't help it, I'm just so happy."

"Me too, now let's go find my dad."

More graduates and their families were starting to arrive, and the field house was starting to bustle and percolate with activity. We had no idea where Keith was. He wasn't answering his cell phone and we didn't know where to meet him. We started heading toward an exit to look for him, and wouldn't you know it, just as we were heading out, there was Keith, in a suit and tie heading in the same door with his camera in tow, ready to document it all.

199

We stepped outside into the bright morning sunlight and quickly posed for pictures; me all misty-eyed with a quiet smile on my face, Keith smiling and squinting into the sun, Jared in his cap and gown. We took a few more quick pics and then Jared headed back in the field house to line up and we went to find seats in the arena.

I cried my makeup off at least two more times during the commencement ceremony, starting with the Processional March and seeing Jared enter the arena and take his seat among his graduating class. We had just by luck picked seats that were directly across from him and could make eye contact off and on during the entire ceremony. Row by row, the graduation candidates were ushered to the stage, and one and by one up the stairs, before a standing-room-only crowd and distinguished platform guests—the university's president, college deans, and board of trustees, all bedecked in their academic regalia. Eventually, I heard Jared's name called and watched as he crossed the stage and received his degree, switching the tassel on his mortarboard from right to left. Five long years and it was finally official: he was a college graduate.

When we headed to lunch, our restaurant had a nice quiet table in the corner available for us right away. We joined hands around the table and I fought mightily to control the quaver in my voice as I blessed the food and thanked God for the day. We enjoyed each other's company, chatting quietly over a meal of Caesar salad and shish kebabs. At various times throughout lunch, Jared was presented with a graduation card, and much to his delight, cash. Towards the end, as cream puffs arrived for dessert, I looked at my only child and said what I felt: "I'm walking a little taller today, Son, because of you."

Before Keith left campus to catch a flight for an out-of-town business meeting, the two of us—Mom and Dad—had a moment alone to congratulate each other on a job well done, and it was then that I realized the last time I had felt this tearfully, blissfully happy, was twenty-three years ago—the day our son was born.

Looking back, all of my experiences, the heartache and joy, have brought about a deep-seated mindfulness; an inward focus that has helped me feel centered and at peace. I've rediscovered me, and settled in to a certain contentment in life. I've learned to be okay with myself and not look to others as the sole source of my happiness.

200

I've learned that true happiness is a direct result of the choices we make, and right choices require courage and consistency. Right choices aren't always popular. Right choices aren't always easy. But you can never go wrong doing what is right. How will you know what choice to make? By first asking yourself what really matters most in your life. Then have the confidence to stand firm. Every decision you make honors what you value the most.

Joy and happiness come from knowing who you are, what you stand for, and what you value most. Only you can define that. Whatever it is, go for it. Be strong through every bumpy road and difficult decision. Stay true to what makes your heart sing, and soon you will discover your very own pockets of joy.

In Psalm 23 it says, "*Yea, though I walk through the valley of the shadow of death, I will fear no evil.*" If you remember anything from this book or my story, remember this: even though we will all encounter tough times in our lives, even though we will all find ourselves at some point in the valley, keep walking. Keep walking toward the light. Keep walking toward that which is good and pure. Keep walking toward that which is true and honest. Keep walking, because, as Psalm 23 says, we walk "***through** the valley of the **shadow** of death.*" We all have the ability to walk through something and not remain where we are, if we just keep focusing on the light. In order for something to cast a shadow, as it says in Psalm 23, there has to be a light source, and that light is God. Light always overcomes darkness and that's why I say to you, my dear friend, through every heartache, loss, and fear, keep walking toward the light, because that's where you will find the joy.

I'm about five years old in this family photo.
Kinda obvious which one is me! My dad is so handsome,
my mom, so beautiful. Love my brothers.

The day we brought Jared home.
The look on my face says it all.

Me and my "little man."

At the height of my television career.

Jared was at the finish every time!

For my full photo album, visit pocketsofjoy.com.

ACKNOWLEDGMENTS

I would like to thank God for holding me with His right hand and never letting go during every step of this fantastical journey called life.

I would like to thank my son Jared and my ex-husband Keith for allowing me to share their lives. Jared, you have grown up to be a kind and gracious man and my greatest joy. Without the support of you and your father this book would have never been possible. Thank you both for the encouragement to write and share our story.

Thank you to my parents, Burnie and Bessie Battle. How befitting that the child you would find asleep in her bed surrounded by books would one day become an author. It was you, Mom, who when I was just eleven years old first discovered I had inherited my great-grandmother's talent for writing. You immediately sent me off to creative writing classes, and, well, the rest, as they say, is history. Thank you, Dad, for never letting me give up on my dream. You would always say, "A winner never quits and a quitter never wins."

Thank you to my four brothers, Burnie Jr., Walter, Robert, and Nate, for, well…being brothers, and feigning to be not all that proud of their sister. I'm on to you.

I would like to thank the publishing team at Whitaker House. Many thanks to Acquisitions Consultant Don Milam and Publicist Cathy Hickling for introducing me to the Whitaker family. Thank you, President and CEO Bob Whitaker for believing in me, my story, and my dream. May God continue to bestow abundant blessings upon you and your family. Thank you, Author Liaison Christine Whitaker. From day one, your many words of support and encouragement helped make publishing this book a joyful experience. Thanks to my editor Judith Dinsmore for her gentle demeanor and brilliant insights, which helped polish a beginner's manuscript into something I'm proud to share with the rest of the world.

Thank you to my friend and publicist, Maureen Cahill. You've been there from the start; from my self-publishing days until now, believing in me every step of the way.

Thank you to my author mentors, Dr. Deborah Smith Pegues and Dr. Sam Chand for being such sterling examples of integrity and self-lessness, for never letting me think the worst and always reminding me to take each day as it comes and that all things are possible.

Thank you also to Pam Borton, Dr. Greg Plotnikoff, Janet Conley, Kathleen Cooke, and Caryn Sullivan for your endorsements.

And a very special thank you to Tavis Smiley and Maria Shriver. Though my encounters with each of you were brief, you both showed enough belief and were quick to offer just enough support to help take my career as an author to the next level. I will be forever grateful.

And finally, a special thanks to my faith community; those of you who stayed close and prayed with and for me as I found my way, one gut-wrenching and trying decision at a time. You know who you are. And I know how you stood by me, believed in me, and encouraged me with your prayers, posts, text messages, long phone calls, and kind words. Thank you for acknowledging the gifts God placed within me and for spurring me on to do good works.

Thank you to everyone whose only contribution was to offer encouragement and love, which has touched my soul, rekindled my passion, and shown me the transformative power of having people in your life who truly believe in you—and that dreams, though delayed, can and do come true.

NOTES

Chapter 2: Flying Solo
1. Robert Munsch, *Love You Forever* (Richmond Hill, ON, Canada: Firefly Books, 1995).
2. Psalm 30:5.

Chapter 8: Fullness of Joy
3. Joshua 1:5.
4. Maria Shriver, *Just Who Will You Be* (New York City: Hyperion, 2008), 33.
5. Deuteronomy 30:19.
6. Hebrews 12:2.

Chapter 9: Authenticity
7. Panache Desai, *Discovering Your Soul Signature* (London: Hodder & Stoughton, 2014), 134.
8. John 8:36.

Chapter 10: Service and Generosity
9. Shannon Prather, "Some Minnesota nonprofits ride post-election surge," *Minneapolis StarTribune*, March 7, 2017, http://www.startribune.com/ some-minnesota-nonprofits-ride-post-election-surge/401977615/ (accessed April 20, 2017).
10. Tal Ben-Shahar, Ph.D., *Happier: Learn the Secrets to Daily Joy and Lasting Fulfillment* (New York: McGraw Hill, 2007), 126.
11. Hebrews 10:24.
12. Galatians 6:7.

Chapter 11: Positive Connections
13. Candace V. Love, *No More Narcissists!* (Oakland, CA: New Harbinger Publications, 2016), 3–4.
14. Philippians 4:8.

Chapter 12: Gratitude

15. Josie Robinson, *The Gratitude Jar* (Minneapolis, MN: Wise Ink Creative Publishing, 2015), 30

16. Philippians 4:7.

17. Romans 8:28.

18. Hebrews 11:1.

19. Max Lucado, *You'll Get Through This* (Nashville: Thomas Nelson, 2013), 27.

20. Malachi 2:16.

21. Romans 8:39.

22. Lamentations 3:22–24.

Chapter 13: Self-Care

23. See Judith Orloff, "The Health Benefits of Tears," *Psychology Today*, July 27, 2010, www.psychologytoday.com/blog/emotional-freedom/201007/the-health-benefits-tears (accessed March 5, 2017).

24. See Jenny Anderson, "Economists quantified what sleep deprivation does to mothers' pay and productivity," *Quartz*, February 17, 2017, https://qz.com/912684/economists-quantified-what-sleep-deprivation-does-to-mothers-pay-and-productivity/ (accessed March 5, 2017).

25. See Tom Haberstroh, "Sitting LeBron makes perfect sense," *ESPN*, February 14, 2017, http://www.espn.com/nba/story/_/id/18547955/dnp-rest-makes-perfect-sense-lebron-james (accessed March 5, 2017).

26. Anthony Slater, "Warriors conduct interesting postgame press conferences after loss to Wolves," *The Mercury News*, March 10, 2017, http://www.mercurynews.com/2017/03/10/warriors-cant-chase-down-wolves-in-tiring-loss-in-minnesota/ (accessed March 13, 2017).

27. See Alice Park, "The Sleep Cure," *Time*, February 16, 2017, http://time.com/4672988/the-sleep-cure-fountain-of-youth/ (accessed March 13, 2017).

28. Genesis 1:27; Psalm 139:14.

Chapter 14: Yielding

29. Timothy Keller and Kathy Keller, *The Meaning of Marriage* (New York City: Riverhead Books, 2011), 183–184.

Chapter 15: Forgiveness

30. Marianne Williamson, *Tears to Triumph* (New York City: HarperOne,

2016), 94.

31. Psalm 103:12.

32. Deborah Smith Pegues, *Forgive, Let Go, and Live* (Eugene, OR: Harvest House Publishers, 2015), 101.

33. Henri J. M. Nouwen, *The Return of the Prodigal Son* (New York City: Doubleday, 1992), 130.